Young Writers 2005 POETRY COMPETITION

PLAYGROU...

Let your crea...

ode

limerick   haiku

rhyme

Ballad

My Poems

- Inspirations From Essex

Edited by Heather Killingray

 Young**Writers**

First published in Great Britain in 2006 by:
Young Writers
Remus House
Coltsfoot Drive
Peterborough
PE2 9JX
Telephone: 01733 890066
Website: www.youngwriters.co.uk

SB ISBN 1 84602 354 8

Foreword

Young Writers was established in 1991 and has been passionately devoted to the promotion of reading and writing in children and young adults ever since. The quest continues today. Young Writers remains as committed to the fostering of burgeoning poetic and literary talent as ever.

This year's Young Writers competition has proven as vibrant and dynamic as ever and we are delighted to present a showcase of the best poetry from across the UK. Each poem has been carefully selected from a wealth of *Playground Poets* entries before ultimately being published in this, our thirteenth primary school poetry series.

Once again, we have been supremely impressed by the overall high quality of the entries we have received. The imagination, energy and creativity which has gone into each young writer's entry made choosing the best poems a challenging and often difficult but ultimately hugely rewarding task - the general high standard of the work submitted amply vindicating this opportunity to bring their poetry to a larger appreciative audience.

We sincerely hope you are pleased with our final selection and that you will enjoy *Playground Poets - Inspirations From Essex* for many years to come.

Contents

George Manley (8)	11
Katharine Rushen (8)	12
Daniel Perry (8)	12
Zahra Gohrabian (8)	12
Edward Baldry (8)	13
Abigail Seakens (8)	13
Hannah Warren (8)	13
Jessica Bradbrook (8)	14

Hamilton Primary School
Poppy Wickenden (9)	14
Tara Pomery (7)	15
Elsa van Helfteren (8)	15
Lily Morgan (7)	16
Melissa Armstrong (7)	16

Lawford CE Primary School
Thekla Kenneison (8)	17
Dionne Laccohee (8)	17
Edward Greenwood (9)	18
Edward Lee (9)	18
Kathleen Johnson (8)	18
Lewis Roberts (10)	19
Katie Farrow (8)	19
Megan Roberts (10)	19
James Crisell (9)	20
Beth Greenwood (9)	20
Michael Shaikly (9)	20
Jack Steed (10)	21
Reshea Taylor (9)	21
Neil Lofts (9)	21
Emily Lane (10)	22
Joe Judson (9)	22
Rebekah Ivell (10)	23
Ruth Everett (9)	23
Luke Bartlett (9)	24
Nathan Archer (9)	24
Naomi Gee (9)	24
Rhiannon Moore (9)	25
Kelly Aherne (10)	25
Jessica Gilray (9)	26

Alice Curtis (10)	26
Claire Osborne (9)	26
Chris Smith (10)	27
Darcy Levison (9)	27
Chelsea Nicholson (10)	28
Rosie Moore (9)	28
Danielle Crouch (10)	29
Alex Garrad (10)	29
Ryan Hynes (10)	29
Jodie Aherne (8)	30
Zoe Bowers (10)	30
Ben Kennell (10)	31
Lucy Everett (11)	31
Anthony Chittock (10)	32
Kirsty Nicholass (10)	32
Kaleigh Bligh (10)	32
Raymond C Cunningham (11)	33
Aaron Edwards (8)	33
Rhys Gooch (11)	33
Chloe Gilbert (10)	34
Katie Cook (10)	34
Hester Kenneison (10)	34
Jodie Norton (10)	35
Gemma Farrow (10)	35
Ottillie Wakley-Johnston (8)	36
Cameron Langford (8)	36
Katherine Drew (8)	37
Jessica Yule (10)	37
Katie Smith (8)	38
Megan Kennell (8)	38
Joshua Harbach (8)	39

Maldon Court Preparatory School

Claire Winder (9)	39
Jessica Rome (9)	40
Harry Hinkins (9)	40
Ellie Quy (10)	41
Olivia Woolnough (8)	41
Jack Bailey (11)	42
Henri Skeens (8)	42
Annie Cousins (10)	43

Montgomery Junior School

St Edward's CE Primary School, Romford

Samuel Cooke (9)	62
Jessica Lord (7)	63
Michael Nance (9)	63
Michael Swan (9)	63
George Swallow (8)	63
Hannah Staggs (10)	64
Elizabeth Tran (10)	64
Elena Sheridan (9)	64
Tiffany Afoké (10)	65
Esther Ojo (7)	65
Beau Lyons (9)	66
Sarah-Jade Stewart (8) & Georgina Every (7)	66
Lucy Andrean (9)	66
Folasade Cline-Thomas (8)	67
Benjamin Paisley (7)	67
Laura Johnson (7)	67
Jessica Pitts (9)	68
Mez Boateng (8)	68
Malanda Cowley (9)	69
Samuel Gowland (8)	69
Corrin Lacey (9)	69
Joseph Powell (10)	70
Katherine Miller (9)	70
Rhiannon Townson (10)	71
Sophie Hughes (9)	71
Joel Oyelese (9)	72
Phoebe Leung (9)	72
Daniel Haynes (10)	73
Modupe Olagundoye (9)	73
Courtney Howell (10)	74
Lauren Angus-Larkin (9)	74
Kenneth Omole (10)	75
Kearney Mott (11)	75
Regan Mott (9)	75
Alexandra Wood (9)	76
Siân West (9)	76
Rowan Barnes (9)	76
Anthony Wise (10)	77
Bethaney Hall (10)	77
Abigail Howson (10)	78
Lauren Kaufman (10)	78
Claire Jackson (10)	79

Jade Hearn (10)	79
Rachel Stewart (10)	80
Thomas Harvey (10)	80
Elsie Lawrence (10)	81
Liam Wheeler (10)	81
Thomas Greene (10)	81
Charlotte Tibbott (10)	82
Arabella Weymouth (10)	82
Elizabeth McDonald (10)	83
Jessica-Rose Spong (9)	83
Daisy Harper (10)	84
Rianna Veares (10)	84
Elise Herring (10)	85
Charlie Turner (8)	85
Lynden Reed (8)	86
Joshua Barnes (10)	86
Axton Reed (8)	87
Hannah Lauder (11)	87
Cecily Henman (11)	88
Henry Eades (10)	88
William Fenton (10)	89
Luke McClenaghan (8)	89
Joshua Dunning (10)	89
Lily Sharpe (8)	90
Tom Read (10)	90
Rachel Phelan (8)	91
Harriet Blowers (8)	91
Rosie Jennings (8)	91
Georgina Allen (9)	92
Katie Butler (11)	92
Emma Cottrell (10)	93
Hope Joanne Garnish (9)	93
Faye Martin (10)	94
Zoe Corbin (8)	94
Oliver Haynes (10)	95
Aiden Jackson (8)	95
Rebecca Staggs (8) & Grace Pawley (7)	95
Kelvin Rushbrook (10)	96
Bradwell John (7)	96
Jodi Whitehead & Palvy Manduakila (7)	96
Dominic Phillips (8)	97
Samuel Kelly (9)	97

Vanessa Hamilton (9)	113
Naomi Vallance (8)	113
Bradley West (7)	113
Jasmine Jennings (7)	113
Charlotte Wickens (7)	114
Daniel Balli (7)	114
Bethany Moore (7)	114
Annabel Webb (8)	114
Maria Marks (10)	115
Joel Poultney (10)	115
Sean Melpuss (10)	116
Alana Speakman-Bell (10)	116
Oyinkansola Sunmonu (10)	117
Callum James (10)	117
Daisy Loomes (10)	118
Amy Morrison (9)	118
Sophie Tibbott (7)	118
James Weimer (10)	119
Robert Carter (9)	119
Katharine Leonard (10)	119
Zachary Trott (10)	120
Lewis Huff (10)	120
Callum Haxell (10)	121
Dominic Cheung (9)	121
Rosie Webber (8)	122
Alex Cutmore (9)	122
Rosie Louise White (9)	122
Christopher Attridge (8)	123
Hannah King (9)	123
Elizabeth Gregory (9)	123
Temi Abatan (8)	124
Fraser Scott (7)	124
Betsey Benson (9)	125
Emmanuel Olusanya (9)	125
Kimberley Stirk (8)	125
Kerrie Norris (8)	126
George Zuber (9)	126
Aimee Harvey (8)	127
Rachael John (7)	127
Adam Ward (8)	128
Liam Chesney (8)	128
Thomas Steer (8)	129

Abbie Legallienne (9)	143
Saffron Robins (9)	143
Ben Austin (9)	144
Gemma Willson (9)	144
Amy Picknell (7)	144
Bruce Beckett (9)	145
Karen Morris (8)	145
Joshua Amofah (7)	145
Sophie Doyle (10)	146

The Bishops' CE & RC (VA) Primary School

Jessica Stephenson (9)	146
Saad Malik (10)	147
Ellie Fivash (10)	147
Joshua Fresle (9)	147
John Akomolafe (9)	148
Olivia Robinson (9)	148
Ellen Battye (9)	149
Rebecca Scott (9)	149
Phoebe Scherer (9)	150
Samuel Ashford (9)	150
Frances Stacey (9)	151
Ashley Lumayag (10)	152
Anna Birmingham (7)	152
Peter Bowdidge (9)	153
Shannon O'Sullivan (9)	153
Megan Norrington (10)	154
Matthew Allen (9)	154
Louise Palmer (9)	154
Bethany Lodge (9)	155
Alex Woolnough (9)	155
Joseph Brenchley (9)	155
Ella Beadel (10)	156
Caitlin Sheehan (9)	156
Courtney Burnette (10)	156
Esther Daniel (9)	157
Georgia Hammond (10)	157
Sinead Collins (10)	157
Sophie Parker (7)	158
Abigail Mariner (9)	158

The Poems

Killer Sun

Dragon Sun scorches the Earth.
Blazing smoke smashes the planet, to red-hot ashes.
Dragon's breath threatens the atmosphere
With balls of smoky fire,
Clenching his claws into the ground,
Ripping it apart, leaving no remains.
Roaring to the sun and smashing it to shreds,
Waiting for the best moment to strike at the planet.

Thomas Pullen (10)
Barling Magna Primary School

Dragon Sun

Burns the spherical planet,
His colossal, whipping, scaly tail injures the land on its feet,
Blowing fireballs at the people on the Earth,
He roars, deafening the entire planet,
Fiery breath dehydrates every living thing he sees,
Even out of the corner of his eye,
Dragon Sun may object to you.

Ben Larkin (9)
Barling Magna Primary School

Falcon Sun

Falcon Sun soars in the sky
Threatening to burn anyone that he finds.
Destroying the trees when he swoops down to kill.
Glinting feathers shine gold,
When he comes down to injure,
Screeching to his fellow falcons as he comes to rest in his nest.

Rebecca Withams (9)
Barling Magna Primary School

Devil Sun

Devil Sun whips the Earth with blazing heat
Injuring anyone who looks at it.
Lashing, clashing and burning all who try to touch.
Playing with fire, like there is nothing to worry about,
Dropping it on Earth when it is time for summer.
Threatens people with its scorching tail of whipping fire,
Waiting for the perfect moment to strike.
It darkens you when it is time for him to rest from fire.

Matthew Higgs (10)
Barling Magna Primary School

Dragon Sun

Dragon Sun burns the Earth,
Torturing it with his fire breath,
Whipping it with his immense tail,
This colossal creature destroying the planet,
Threatening the land as he roars,
Killing the plants as he guzzles the water.

Kate Ruston (10)
Barling Magna Primary School

Dragon Sun

Dragon Sun scorches the Earth with his fiery breath,
Dragon Sun dazzles a human's eye,
Dragon Sun wounds an animal with his colossal tail,
Dragon Sun drinks water from a fast-flowing river,
Dragon Sun exhausts everyone on the Earth,
Dragon Sun kills the plants with his sharp claws.

Amber Everson (10)
Barling Magna Primary School

Tiger Sun

Tiger Sun, scrapes his claws across his prey,
Tumbles the Earth as he pounces about,
Whips his tail as he threatens the creatures surrounding him,
Kills you with his deafening roar.
His mouth watering as he chews with his jaws,
Blazing hot as he walks to his prey,
The sun sizzling like a baking oven.

Lauren Keen (10)
Barling Magna Primary School

Lion Sun

The Lion Sun burns with its golden mane,
As it grows nearer and nearer to you
You start to sweat like mad,
You can hear it roar as it circles you ready to attack.
You feel like running away
But it seems like your feet are glued to the floor.
You get hotter and hotter as you stare into its eyes.

Alice Cook (9)
Barling Magna Primary School

Sun

The Dragon Sun spins dangerously,
Ready to burn and destroy,
It's coming to harm all living things,
Ready to whip with its wings,
It's hot and deadly,
Ready to breathe fire and kill.

Jack Pluthero
Barling Magna Primary School

Lion Predator

Lion Sun pounces on its prey,
It's sure to die by the end of the day.
I bet it's going to kill something,
Of course because it's the Animal King.
Its mane is a ball of fire,
On the food chain nothing is higher.
Its roar makes you deaf,
One hit and it's your death.
Leaving fire in its wake,
Rain falls so it doesn't bake.
They want the power of the sun, like a raging lion,
Like a predator, like the king.

Charles Butler (10)
Barling Magna Primary School

Lion Sun

Lion Sun threatens the Earth with sharp, angry fiery claws,
Kills and eats tiny, scared creatures which are desperate for water,
Deafens you with his loud killing moan,
Torturing and whips his tail and demolishes the town,
His sizzling hot, fiery breath blows fire on the Earth,
Wounding trees and flowers.

Stacie Smith (10)
Barling Magna Primary School

Dragon Sun

Dragon Sun burns the Earth,
Wounds the atmosphere with red-hot fire.
Dazzling sun whips the ground with its deadly tail.
Dragon kills nature by blowing his fire with blazing flames.

Hollie Jobson (10)
Barling Magna Primary School

Dragon Sun

Dragon Sun burning the Earth to the core,
Killing all living creatures in its gaze.
Drinking all the water out of the ground,
A massive spherical fireball suffocating the Earth.

Whipping the world with its fiery tail,
Torturing the planet with its ear-piercing roar,
Torturing the world with its blazing breath,
Killing the people, blowing fireballs,
Ripping the universe apart.

Oliver Woodhouse (9)
Barling Magna Primary School

Dragon Sun

Dragon Sun heating all of the Earth,
Drinking all moisture in the air,
Burning me as I sunbathe,
My skin was like crispy bacon.
Dehydrates everyone as the sun beats down on everyone,
Neighbours sizzling hot, burning like the sun.

Demi-Louise McGovern (9)
Barling Magna Primary School

Dragon Sun

Dragon Sun kills you with its fiery beam,
Takes plants' water as they grow,
Burning your skin till it hurts,
Blinds creatures with its light,
Starved of coldness, freezing trees,
Everyone burning like crispy bacon.

Megan Linsdell (10)
Barling Magna Primary School

Dragon Sun

Dragon Sun destroys the Earth with his flaming breath,
Threatens us as he whips his blistering tail,
Dehydrates people with the scorching heat.
Dragon Sun kills the plants as he drinks their water given to them,
He exhausts living creatures and humans with blazing flames.

Briony Ball (10)
Barling Magna Primary School

Sun Dragon

Dragon Sun dazzles the Earth with his whipping tail,
Threatening to scorch the ground
And to kill all enemies in sight.
If you are in his path, you will be in awesome danger,
You need to be aware and keep your foot in line!

Harry Cornwell (11)
Barling Magna Primary School

Dragon Sun

Dragon Sun beats your skin with blazing whips of fire,
As he beams on the land, the people scream
With fright when things go up in smoke-filled flames,
When the plants dehydrate and the water disappears
And everything, so does the world.

Ben Green (10)
Barling Magna Primary School

Dragon Sun

Dragon Sun burns the Earth,
As it smashes the planet hotter than dragon's breath.
It hits the Earth like a blinding ball of fire.
The scorching sun beams on the grass like a fireball.

Jack McClune (10)
Barling Magna Primary School

Dragon Sun

Dragon Sun burning all of the Earth,
Drinking all the moisture in the air.
Fiery tail deserting the world,
Killing and striking at any time.
Boiling hot flames beating down on my back,
Everyone sizzling like crispy bacon.

Faye Brumby (9)
Barling Magna Primary School

Dragon Sun

Dragon Sun burns the Earth with his blazing breath,
He scorches every living creature in sight,
He makes the planet a fireball with his scorching flaming mouth
And he boils everything in his path.

Jack Tarbuck (10)
Barling Magna Primary School

Dragon Sun

Dragon Sun scares the creatures,
Kills you with his fiery breath.
Wounds plants by licking the cold water,
Heats the land with his mild flames.

Hayley Carlton (9)
Barling Magna Primary School

Devil Sun

Devil Sun harms you with his blazing tail,
Killing anyone that walks in his fiery path,
Parched, arid land for miles around,
Withered up lakes and ponds where he shines,
Burning up the atmosphere when he flies around.

Hannah Gardiner (10)
Barling Magna Primary School

Dragon Sun

Dragon Sun, roars at the Earth,
Threatens the planet as he whips his fiery tail,
Dazzles his friends as he wounds the plants,
Killing the trees as he guzzles up the water,
Burns your skin as you sunbathe.

Hollie Haynes (10)
Barling Magna Primary School

Killer Sun

Dragon Sun burns the Earth,
He whips the petals off the plants,
He exhausts the children running around
And kills living creatures on the ground.
He kills the winter so it's summer
And shines on the sea so it glistens.

Gina Kirby (10)
Barling Magna Primary School

Dragons

Sending mushroom-shaped fire clouds into the sky,
Silvery-blue slashing tails and stamping feet,
Smooth, scaled green backs,
Red odd fringes of fine gold spikes,
Vicious-looking black fanged mouths bursting enormous fiery rockets,
Gigantic torrents of fire,
With their huge flapping wings beaming yellow in the sky.

Chloe Swayne (10)
Cherry Tree Primary School

Racism

They teased me in the playground,
Laughed at me out of school.
I tried to control myself,
Not to let out a roar.

It's not my fault that I'm different,
My mum says it's a gift.
They don't think that though,
But I've got the secret,
That wraps me inside myself.

It's not my fault that I'm a different colour,
It's not like it's a disease.
I'm trying to learn their language,
But I'm not the bee's knees.

I'm going to use the secret,
When they come near.
And when I've used the secret,
They'll look at me in fear.

Matthew Canham (10)
Cherry Tree Primary School

What Am I?

My first is in snail but not in whale.
My second is in monkey but not in rabbit.
My third is in ant but not in fly.
My fourth is in koala and also in kangaroo.
My last is in turtles but not in frog.
Sometimes I slither and also might bite you.

What am I?
A: A snake.

Charlie Shute (10)
Cherry Tree Primary School

What Am I?

My first is in broccoli but not in onion,
My second is in peppermint but not in pasta.
My third is in naan bread and also in pizza,
My last is in knife but not in fork.

A: A bean.

Rhiannon Ware (9)
Cherry Tree Primary School

Rhino Poem

Rhino, rhino, pink and yellow,
Rhino, orange and purple.
Rhino, rhino, nice and juicy,
Rhino fat, rhino chubby.
Rhino nice, rhino mean,
Rhino angry, fierce and lean.
Football rhino, rugby rhino,
Cricket rhino, tennis rhino.
Rhino famous, rhino basketball player,
Rhino champion in his league.

Connor Wilkinson (7)
Danbury Park Primary School

The Sea

The sea sways
As it sloshes in the bays.
The sea is calm
Like a fragile palm.
The sea prances
And also dances.
The sea swirls
Like swishing pearls.

Catherine Bucknell (8)
Danbury Park Primary School

The Castle Wall

The army is approaching,
Get up on the wall,
You must be very careful
Otherwise you'll fall.
Pick up all your weapons,
Get ready to attack,
Fill up all the catapults
With heads in a sack.
Get the king in armour,
Protect him with a knight,
Also get the soldiers
And prepare to fight.

Alex Sammons (7)
Danbury Park Primary School

You Should Listen To The Old Grey

You should listen to the grey,
They might have wise things to say.
They might be old,
They might even be older,
But you should still listen to the grey,
They might have wise things to say.

Joshua Wheal (8)
Danbury Park Primary School

A Poem For Footie Fans Everywhere

Footie is my passion, I give it my all,
The true romance in my life is eleven men and a ball.
The reason I wrote this poem is cos
I'm football crazy and all!

George Manley (8)
Danbury Park Primary School

Polar Bear

Polar bear,
Happy bear,
Baby bear,
Father bear,
Acting bear,
Sad bear,
Detective bear,
Jungle bear,
Talent bear,
Football bear.
If you like all of these bears
Why not play football with them!

Katharine Rushen (8)
Danbury Park Primary School

The Slow Tortoise

Tortoises are always slow
And when they're in a race they always lose.
When they're brothers and sisters they fight over who's the biggest,
They never get fed up of fighting.
When they get to a hundred they don't get a letter from the Queen,
They're not big and tough,
But most of all they're the slowest animals I've seen.

Daniel Perry (8)
Danbury Park Primary School

Cucumbers

I like cucumbers, they are green and tasty.
I like cucumbers because they are round and so tasty.
I like cucumbers, but the only thing that I don't like about them
Is that they are green and I don't like the colour green.

Zahra Gohrabian (8)
Danbury Park Primary School

Willy Wonka

Willy Wonka spied a conker hanging from a tree.
Willy Wonka to his conker hee, hee, hee, hee, hee.
He reached up high, pulled it down and holed it through with string,
Then went off to play a game, what luck it was to bring.
He hit it hard, an almighty smash sent all his friends away,
His friends all cheered as he did win the conker bash that day!

Edward Baldry (8)
Danbury Park Primary School

Untitled

I've got a kitten, he is black,
He really loves to play around.
He is cute and fluffy.
I love him so, except when he scratches and bites my toe.
He chases his mouse and crosses the house.

Abigail Seakens (8)
Danbury Park Primary School

Lions

Lions are stalking round, looking for something to eat.
If you don't run quite fast enough, you'll turn into dead meat.
They're looking, they're watching, they're smelling all around,
You shouldn't watch or wonder, or even make a sound.
They're running now so fast and leaping through the air,
Claws stretched out to pounce and tear and catch you unaware.
They've got you now, grasped in their claws . . .

Hannah Warren (8)
Danbury Park Primary School

Henry

My little brother is sometimes naughty
And sometimes he is good as gold,
Sometimes he's a joy,
Sometimes he's a pain
But he is always brave and bold.

We play fun games of hide-and-seek
And always have good times,
But when he is tired
He sits on my knee
And I sing him nursery rhymes.

Jessica Bradbrook (8)
Danbury Park Primary School

What I Hear At Night-Time

Tap drips, drips, *drip-drop.*
Loo flushes *flush, flush, flush.*
Mystery footsteps creeping on the landing.
Chattering voices - ones I don't know.
Washing machine woshy and wishy.
Snoring sister *zzzzzz.*
Window opens with great flurry,
Dustbin rattles in a tune.
Stormy plane zooms by.
Leaves patter against my window.
Squawking owl high up in the tree.
Rain drips down the drainpipe.
Hear my neighbour's music.
Slowly fall asleep . . .

Poppy Wickenden (9)
Hamilton Primary School

A Stormy Bonfire Night

Leaves rustling against my window -
Long, dark shadows.
The shining moon glistening through my window.
Blind voice from my mum and dad downstairs.
People rushing along the creaking landing to get to bed.
Black lining along the tops of the houses.
Army men shooting from across the road.
TV constantly chatting,
Car headlights flashing.
Trees swaying in the pitch-black sky.
Crowds shouting,
Fires crackling loudly.
Fireworks flashing out of the blackness,
Lighting up my room.

Tara Pomery (7)
Hamilton Primary School

Rain

Rain is raining all around,
Down through space and to the ground.
What a great sound!
Puddles getting bigger and bigger,
Then emerge into a figure.

It is me.

People safe inside
Watching the weather forecast
As it lied -
And the rain as it flew by.

Elsa van Helfteren (8)
Hamilton Primary School

The Storm

The storm shouting overhead,
Then whistling in a squeaky voice.
Bright flashing
That fills my room
As though my light has been
Quickly switched
On and off.
It makes me jump!
Faces on my curtains,
The leaves become hair,
The eyes look cross
And the mouths are wide
And full of teeth.
I tuck under my sheet
And feel the softness on me.

Lily Morgan (7)
Hamilton Primary School

Walking In The Rain

The rain tips on my raincoat
And when my mum says get in it makes me jump.
It patters on the ground.
Pitch-black trees with long, long branches
And large trunks with very dark marks.
Rolling bins in the gardens,
People's music playing loud in the distance.

Melissa Armstrong (7)
Hamilton Primary School

The Deer And The Cheetah

A deer was hiding in the grass,
Knowing that it was fast,
Suddenly a cheetah sprang
But the deer had a secret fang.
The cheetah ran round and round,
Coming down to touch the ground,
For it had jumped over a wall,
Leaving the deer at the mall.
But the deer was quite clever,
So it hid in the cellar.
It wanted to lure the cheetah to its trap,
So it could eat some sap.
The next day, the cheetah came,
Feeling just the same.
The deer cried, 'Come over here!'
But the cheetah just gave a sneer.
On the table, the deer placed some meat,
Hoping that the cheetah would eat
So the bolt would fall on its head,
And then the cheetah would be *dead!*

Thekla Kenneison (8)
Lawford CE Primary School

Cats Are The Best

I love cats because they're cuddly.
I love cats because their eyes are as green as grass.
I love cats because they climb on my bed at night.
I love cats, especially my cat.
I love cats, I love cats,
They're the best!

Dionne Laccohee (8)
Lawford CE Primary School

Summer Has Gone

Leaves start to die,
Gloom fills the sky.

A breeze so bitter,
Leaves fall down like a pile of glitter.

Summer was fun,
Now autumn has come.

Leaf colours don't go,
But rainwater will flow.

Summer has gone.

Edward Greenwood (9)
Lawford CE Primary School

Autumn

Summer is out and autumn's about,
The crispy leaves fall from the trees.

The howl of the winds
When autumn begins.

The empty chestnut shells lay on the ground,
Without a trace, without a sound.

The howl of the winds
When autumn begins.

Edward Lee (9)
Lawford CE Primary School

Cats!

Cats are crazy,
Cats are cool,
Cats would rule if they went to school.

Kathleen Johnson (8)
Lawford CE Primary School

Autumn Time

The crisp air feels cold and wet,
Hallowe'en is scary, I bet,
Conkers spinning round and round,
Slowly breaking, then suddenly smash!

Leaves turn amber as well as gold,
It is getting very cold,
All the leaves swirl and whirl,
Like a virus in your head.

Lewis Roberts (10)
Lawford CE Primary School

The Funky Monkey

I saw a monkey swing from a tree,
Jumping all around and itching his fleas.
Pinching bananas from the other monkeys,
They went mad and turned all funky.
He's so furry, brown and sweet,
But just be careful he will nick your treat.

Katie Farrow (8)
Lawford CE Primary School

Autumn

Autumn is here,
The crunchy leaves have fallen,
Conkers are out,
Leaves are fluttering about
In the crisp air.
Leaves are rejected,
Burgundy leaves fall off trees,
See the dizzy leaves swirling about.

Megan Roberts (10)
Lawford CE Primary School

Autumn Has Sprung

Bitter breeze bites through the fur of animals,
As conkers spray off the trees
Summer has gone, autumn has come.

Leaves and branches sway in the breeze,
While the grass is about to freeze,
Children swinging conkers around and having fun.

While leaves are getting rejected and piling on the ground,
The grass is almost leaf-bound.
There is barely a sound.

James Crisell (9)
Lawford CE Primary School

Autumn Has Arrived!

Animals stir and push rejected leaves out of their den,
The emerald grass dotted with gold and scarlet.
Gusts of wind filled with frost and dew lift feeble twigs
And leaves to new destinations.
Glistening chestnuts and conkers rolling across the leaf litter,
As the withered oak drops its dashing load.
The desperate winds try to freeze the children's faces
And try to knock the pine cones off the willow patterned trees.
Autumn has arrived!

Beth Greenwood (9)
Lawford CE Primary School

Autumn

The wind blew as the leaves fluttered to the ground,
Acorns landing with a thump.
The whistle of wind sounded like anger
The air felt so damp.
Children were playing as the wind blew faster and faster,
Conkers in competition, cries of laughter.

Michael Shaikly (9)
Lawford CE Primary School

Autumn Is Here

Crisp leaves fall from the crumbling trees, swifting in the breezy air,
They crunch when trampled feet push on them.
The trees look bare, not colourful anymore.
Hallowe'en spooky, pumpkins glowing, the harvest is here.
Giving food to the poor, caring and sharing,
Autumn is here!

Jack Steed (10)
Lawford CE Primary School

Autumn Poem

Autumn is here
Hallowe'en time - people in scary costumes,
Leaves falling off the trees,
Harvest food for the people with no food,
Grass is wet.
Hedgehogs with spiky backs look for food,
Squirrels collect nuts for the winter,
Trees rejecting all old leaves.

Reshea Taylor (9)
Lawford CE Primary School

Autumn Has Come

Autumn has come,
It's time to be hit by the cold weather,
Pine cones drop and bounce off the ground.

Leaves swirl around,
It makes me dizzy,
I tumble around, kicking the colourful leaves.

Men rake leaves into piles,
Hedgehogs rolling in the leaves in a spiky ball,
When autumn ends, snow will fall.

Neil Lofts (9)
Lawford CE Primary School

Gabriel's Message

'Mary,' said Gabriel,
'You are the chosen one.
The Lord has chosen you of all.'

'Gabriel,' said Mary,
'This cannot be the truth.
I cannot give birth to a child,
I'm barely past my youth!'

'Oh Mary!' said Gabriel.
'You do not understand.
Our God has picked you
Out of every woman in the land.'

'Oh Gabriel, oh Gabriel,
Why, oh why is it me?
I am not worthy of a son,
I am not,' said she.

A star shines brightly in the sky
Twinkling up above
A stable in Bethlehem
Filled with a woman's love.

Mary's had the baby
Mary's given birth
To a baby who will one day be
The greatest man on Earth.

Emily Lane (10)
Lawford CE Primary School

Autumn Poem

The crunchy leaves fly and die,
With wonderful colours that scrape
Along the ground.

Leaves are amber, yellow and gold,
They float and crash into the trees.

Joe Judson (9)
Lawford CE Primary School

Autumn Wonders

Leaves go swirling to the ground,
The park is now filled with sound.

All the children's faces are cold,
There are people, young and old.

Crunchy leaves all over the floor,
The chill in the air makes toes very sore.

Crops are growing extremely fast,
Let's just hope that they will last.

Conkers lay upon the ground,
Sitting and waiting to be found.

Inside chestnut shells are as smooth as silk,
It's as smooth as a cup of milk.

Pine cones are closed up, waiting to fall,
Big ones, medium ones, most of them are small.

Rebekah Ivell (10)
Lawford CE Primary School

Autumn Days

The crisp twirling leaves come to a halt
And as they land on the ground
They're as quiet as a colt.

As eerie Hallowe'en comes close,
There are lots of sayings of ghosts.

The seesaw is rocking,
As the wind is blowing.
The creaking of the roundabout
Sounds like knocking.

It's time for Hallowe'en,
All the trick and treaters are keen,
Everyone gives out sweets
Lots and lots of treats.

Ruth Everett (9)
Lawford CE Primary School

Autumn

Crunchy conkers and leaves,
Conkers bash down and leaves are so gentle,
They flutter and glide down to the ground.

The mist in the forest is beautiful,
With pine cones and fallen leaves on the floor.

It looks like a magical land,
Leaves glide down from wonderful trees,
It sounds so beautiful,
Like the delicate sea, hitting the rocks.

Luke Bartlett (9)
Lawford CE Primary School

Autumn

The crispy leaves fall and smashed onto the ground,
And a few seconds later a conker falls and hits the leaf
It breaks in two and then flies away.

Hallowe'en is on its way
It's only a few days away,
I'm so excited I might explode
I may get some sweets, quite a load.

Nathan Archer (9)
Lawford CE Primary School

Autumn Feelings

Autumn leaves fall soft and slow,
Covering the ground with a brown carpet so nothing can grow.

The air goes misty, steamy and dim,
Sometimes you can see nothing, not a thing.

It's getting chilly, cool also bitter,
Leaves are covering the ground like a natural litter.

Naomi Gee (9)
Lawford CE Primary School

Autumn Breeze

Summer has gone
Autumn is here,
The birds have stopped chirping,
Squirrels have fear.

The leaves are falling,
The sun is low.
The wind is breezy
It has a gentle flow.

Spooky Hallowe'en,
Red, black and green
Are the colours that go with
The monsters that are mean.

The autumn is over,
Winter is here.
My brother is crying now
I have a tear.

Rhiannon Moore (9)
Lawford CE Primary School

Christmas Poem

Treading through the snow
As I wander home
Feeling the wind through my hair
As I wrap my coat around me
I get home and see a Christmas tree
A few presents under there.

I wake up on Christmas morning
And open all my presents
I listen to Christmas music
As I play with my toys.

Happy Christmas.

Kelly Aherne (10)
Lawford CE Primary School

Autumn Is Here

Autumn is here
Leaves of amber, red, yellow and orange,
Leaves fall to the ground, all crispy and crunchy.
Conkers are out.

The ground is damp and it's misty,
Chestnuts and pine cones fall to the ground,
Harvest is coming,
Hallowe'en is too.
Autumn is here.

Jessica Gilray (9)
Lawford CE Primary School

Fishing

As I sit by the peaceful lake
What a great day this will make
On my line I have a maggot
In these cold autumn months, I really need a jacket
Leaves are red, orange, yellow
Beyond the hills there are some meadows
Yes, yes I've caught a fish
Finally I've got my wish.

Alice Curtis (10)
Lawford CE Primary School

Autumn Poem

Autumn leaves swirling down to the ground,
Under the crispy leaves I hear a sound.
Children stand on crunchy leaves,
Leaves blow with the gentle breeze.
Conkers stay put, like they're pinned.
Pine cones lay with golden leaves
Wishing they were big trees.

Claire Osborne (9)
Lawford CE Primary School

Christmas Has Come

C arol singing at your door,
H appy faces on the children.
R especting children all around,
I t's time to get the mince pies ready,
S atisfied faces, I bet you will meet,
T ogether, everyone can have fun.
M erry sounds all around,
A musing presents you could get,
S anta coming down a chimney.

H ysterical children having a snowball fight,
A nd you can join in if you want.
S herry gets drunk during the feast.

C runching across on the floor,
O ld people in the warm.
M erry faces down your street,
E veryone has a merry ending.

Chris Smith (10)
Lawford CE Primary School

The Leaf

The withered leaf falls through the branches
Squirrels watch as it passes.

Spiky conkers overtake it quickly
They can't go slow, they're too prickly.

The north wind races across the sky
The leaf falls closer, closer.

In a trice, it hits the ground
Making a crunch that would make your heart pound.

In among the leaves, the conkers and trees, it fell
Where exactly, no one could tell.

Darcy Levison (9)
Lawford CE Primary School

Friends Forever

Friends are people who trust each other
They always talk things through
They never go behind your back
They think before they 'do'.

They comfort you when you're down
They bring smiles your way,
They're there for you and
That's what friends are for.

When you break up with your friends
They say there's a reason,
They say that time will heal
But neither time nor reason
Will change the way you feel.

Chelsea Nicholson (10)
Lawford CE Primary School

Autumn Days

Swirling leaves turning round and round
Carefully landing on the damp ground
Bouncing in the crunching leaves
Crunch, crisp, orange, red, yellow
Brown and burgundy.
Conkers, pine cones and chestnuts, brown
Big trees bare in the cold air.
Scary costumes beware!
Collect candy at people's doors, it's Hallowe'en
Harvest Festival gives food
For people who haven't got tasty food like us.
Nearly winter,
It's autumn, hooray!

Rosie Moore (9)
Lawford CE Primary School

Christmas

C hristmas is a good time of year
H appy Christmas, they always say to me
R eindeer are a cute Christmas animal
I always feel excited and very happy
S anta is a kind man who leaves me stuff to be happy
T oast we leave for Santa because he'll be hungry
M erry Christmas to everyone and a happy New Year
A ngels sing as Santa brings the gifts
S anta is a nice man, so merry Christmas to you!

Danielle Crouch (10)
Lawford CE Primary School

Football Poem

David Beckham running down the pitch,
But a glitch awaits
Him at the other end of the pitch.
Penalties, penalties! Players at the penalty spot.
Michael Owen shoots and misses.
Ronaldinho hisses to better luck next time.
Red card, red card, red card! Players going to the bench.
Blow! the match has ended.

Alex Garrad (10)
Lawford CE Primary School

The World Of Dreams

Bad dreams make you agitated,
Good dreams make you happy.
Evil dreams make you scared,
Well-behaved dreams make you happier,
Violent dreams make you sleep-talk.
Frightening dreams make you wake up,
And worst of all, nightmares!

Ryan Hynes (10)
Lawford CE Primary School

My Little Kitten

My little kitten
Is a cheeky little kitten
She's cute and her name is Kira.
She comes up to your room
To give you a hug,
She puts her neck under yours
She's all furry and cuddly.
She gives you a scratch,
Because she likes playing.
My little kitten
Has to have a tablet,
She has a split in her side.
She loves food
She can eat for England,
She likes pouncing,
She loves my family.
She gives me a kiss on the lips
Before I go to school.
She loves everyone in my family
And that's my little kitten!

Jodie Aherne (8)
Lawford CE Primary School

Zoe Bowers

Z oe is my name
O h my mum and dad, I love them so
E ndless love for my family

B rothers, I have three of them
O verall I have a loving family
W hen I'm glum, they cheer me up
E very day my mum wakes me up with a smile
R acing my brother, I sometimes win, but it's always fun
S omersaulting in the garden with my three brothers.

Zoe Bowers (10)
Lawford CE Primary School

Battlefields

Running around the battlefield frantically
Bullets flying everywhere.

People falling to the ground
The green grass there once was,
Is now covered by dead bodies.

Bombs flying everywhere
Making craters, killing men.

Enemy rushing forward
Allies retreating.

One army celebrating
The other on the floor
Begging for their lives.

Ben Kennell (10)
Lawford CE Primary School

Farmyard Animals

Rats scurry around the barn,
Cats prowl across the farm.
Chickens cluck and eat the corn,
Dogs chase balls across the lawn.

Cows moo and chew the cud,
Pigs love to roll in the mud.
Lambs hop and skip around the field,
Mice eat the farmer's yield.

Ponies nicker and canter across the ground,
Geese squawk and make a terrible sound.
Goats are greedy and like to eat,
Ducks will sometimes munch on wheat.

Lucy Everett (11)
Lawford CE Primary School

Abseiling

A lways wear your harness and helmet,
B e wary, there are loose rocks.
S o are you ready to start?
E verybody beware there are others abseiling.
I f a rope snaps, try to continue,
L ook at the outstanding view.
I t's time to head for the ground,
N ow you're halfway down.
G round, you did it, you abseiled.

Anthony Chittock (10)
Lawford CE Primary School

Christmas

Christmas is coming soon
I walk through the woods in the crispy leaves
The snow begins to fall
The dew is glistening
And the snow is too
A scary figure jumps out of a tree
It really scared me
Guess what?
It was my annoying brother.

Kirsty Nicholass (10)
Lawford CE Primary School

My Dog, Coco

C hocolate: her coat is a lovely chocolate-brown,
O bviously excited, whenever I see her she shows excitement.
C areless: she knocks over lots of things,
O ptimistic: she's always cheerful.
        I love my dog, Coco.

Kaleigh Bligh (10)
Lawford CE Primary School

Farm Sleeping

Cute cats sleeping on the lawn,
dreaming of days yet to come.

Pigs sleeping in their sty
wondering what life is like with a human eye.

Cows asleep in the field,
dreaming of the cud they will eat.

Sheepdogs asleep by the fire,
dreaming about herding the sheep.

Farmer, sleeping in his bed,
dreaming about . . . well, we just don't know.

Raymond C Cunningham (11)
Lawford CE Primary School

Reckless Rally Cars

Rally cars race super quick
They bash about,
Bits fall off them.
The mud goes everywhere,
Engines roar recklessly.
Flames whizz through the exhaust
With acceleration!

Aaron Edwards (8)
Lawford CE Primary School

Sports

S printing
P ersevere
O rienteering
R acing
T rying
S porty.

Rhys Gooch (11)
Lawford CE Primary School

Hallowe'en

Bats come out at Hallowe'en
Aliens run and scream,
Witches are spotted and seen
All on Hallowe'en.

Experimental werewolves howling at the moon,
Skeletons come out, very soon.
UFOs fly in the sky, very high
All on Hallowe'en.

Chloe Gilbert (10)
Lawford CE Primary School

The Snowy Morning Of Christmas Eve

On Christmas Eve,
I like to play in the snow with my brother,
We have snow fights during the week.
Counting down the days to the number one day of the year.
Then it comes, Christmas Eve,
With marshmallows and cream with a flake
And hot chocolate.
The best day of the year.

Katie Cook (10)
Lawford CE Primary School

Acorns To Oaks

From the tiny acorn
To the oak tree, big and strong,
And may there be implanted
A fairy from the throng.
And may its heart be full of love
For the oak tree alone,
And may its fairy dances
Help the plants grow.

Hester Kenneison (10)
Lawford CE Primary School

Hallowe'en

Monsters come out at Hallowe'en
Little children run and scream.
Children rotting their teeth with sweets
At Hallowe'en.
Witches fly on Hallowe'en,
Witches cast spells on little children
At Hallowe'en.

Mummies come alive at Hallowe'en
Little children get mummified
At Hallowe'en.
The world is a horrible place
Nobody wants to be in the world
At Hallowe'en.

Jodie Norton (10)
Lawford CE Primary School

A Sunlit Day

S un twinkling onto the moving sea,
U mbrellas are not needed and are turning dusty.
N umberless people laying in the gleaming sun.
L oaded towns, packed full of joyfulness,
I ts sizzling heat, sends rays to the ground.
T ime quickly running away,

D rying clothes is now not a chore.
A musement gathers and everyone is ecstatic.
Y esterday is now over, let's hope it comes again.

Gemma Farrow (10)
Lawford CE Primary School

Pets

You can get all kinds of pets
But if you choose the wrong one
Your house could become
A complete pit
So take my advice
And choose the right one.
If you get a cat
Don't get a rat
If you get a mouse
Don't let it in the house
So those are the rules for pets.

Ottillie Wakley-Johnston (8)
Lawford CE Primary School

Medicinal Compound!

Cheetahs are cheating
Snails are sick
The koalas are kissing
This happened so quick!
I don't know what to do
And guess what?
The panthers are panting
The lions are lying
And the cure is
Medicinal compound!

Cameron Langford (8)
Lawford CE Primary School

Woodland Animals

In a lovely woodland,
A woodland so very calm.
The calmness was broken by a sound,
A squirrel in a hurry,
Then it was silent until it was broken yet again.
But this time it wasn't a squirrel in a hurry,
It was a deer as quick as a dart,
Knowing that it would be late.
It was silent until a noise came,
But not a squirrel or a deer,
Because it was a mouse coming close.
'Where are they all off to?' I wonder,
I think I know.
I expect they're going to an
Animal meeting!

Katherine Drew (8)
Lawford CE Primary School

Hot-Air Balloon

Flying up
towards the
clouds, being
followed by people
down below, feeling the
breeze rush through
my hair, gliding
gently towards
the
ground.

Jessica Yule (10)
Lawford CE Primary School

The Naughty Bunny

The cheeky rabbit was naughty all day,
When he went to the shops, he didn't pay.
He ate my grass
But he didn't run fast.
When I came to the door,
He hit me on the head with an oar.
My head was sore
And then he threw an apple core.
Guess what, I said,
'You naughty bunny, go to bed!'

Katie Smith (8)
Lawford CE Primary School

Have You Ever Seen?

Have you ever seen a flying fish?
Have you ever seen a mouse in a dish?
Have you? Have you?
Have you ever seen a dog doing karate?
Have you ever seen a mouse go to a party?
Have you? Have you?
Have you ever seen the terrible twins?
Have you ever seen a frog with wings?
Have you? Have you?

Megan Kennell (8)
Lawford CE Primary School

My Dog

My dog
Always
Catches
Flies
Every day.
My dog
Always
Tries to
Catch
My neighbour's cat's tail!

Joshua Harbach (8)
Lawford CE Primary School

A Trip To The Seaside

I am very excited, I'm going to the sea,
First I will have my cup of tea,
I drink it and we're off to the seaside to see the sea,
Lots of sand and sunshine.
My brother and I are building a castle
And it will be the best on the beach.
We are heading for the sea,
My brother catches a wave,
There's one coming up,
I catch it,
We're heading for the shore,
'Oh no,' it's going to pour,
We run back to our stuff,
Grab it and head for home,
It was a lovely day, I would do it again.

Claire Winder (9)
Maldon Court Preparatory School

Birthday Parties

Birthday parties are a lot of fun
There're biscuits and cake for everyone.
There're musical games that children enjoy,
But watch out for those rowdy boys!
Colourful presents, big and small
Given by children, short and tall.
In the corner there's a magic man
We knew he was here, because of his van.
The room is filled with balloons and streamers
There's even a piñata that looks like a lemur
And now it's time for the big surprise
The lights got out, I can't believe my eyes!
In comes mum with the birthday cake
It's long and wiggly, it looks like a snake
Now the children go home, back to teddy
The cake's all gone and there's no more jelly
But all you children, make no mistake,
If you eat too much cake you will
Get a stomach ache.

Jessica Rome (9)
Maldon Court Preparatory School

Winter Awakes

As the dawns grow darker
And the nights a thickening black,
The owls hoot an echoing sound,
The howling wind whooshes past.
You see the glistening stars much better,
The moon is a ball of light,
This my friend, is the winter awakening.

Harry Hinkins (9)
Maldon Court Preparatory School

Autumn

The trees are swaying in the wind,
It is autumn again.
The leaves are turning yellow, orange and red,
You can hear the birds singing as they go to bed.
The days are getting colder, conkers are falling,
Children are collecting and playing and calling.
Everyone is dressing up for Hallowe'en,
Witches, wizards, vampires and bats,
All scary things like witches' cats.
Bonfire night is so exciting,
Fire, lights and candlesticks shining brightly.
Fireworks banging loud,
High up in the sky,
Shining brightly, sparkling, shimmering
And then they die.

Ellie Quy (10)
Maldon Court Preparatory School

School Stuff

I like football
Because playtime never ends,
I love to play and call and shout!
Especially with my friends.

I'm going to enjoy my lunch today
Because my tummy is making noises.
Afterwards I'll go out and play!
And sing, 'Ring O' Ring O' Roses'.

The clock is ticking round and round
And literacy is nearly over,
I would rather watch the bees,
Go picking at the clover!

Olivia Woolnough (8)
Maldon Court Preparatory School

The Pool Game

The stadium lights go on,
The triangle is set,
The cues are chalked,
The match begins.

Bailey breaks, a red goes down,
Walder shocked, Bailey looks at the balls,
He's about to hit, he just missed the blue,
But hits the green!

Walder's turn, he hits, it goes in,
He hits another, it goes in
And another and in,
Bailey's in real shock.

Each player's down to two balls,
Bailey hits, it goes down,
He hits again and it is in,
Just the black, he's missed.

Walder hits and in,
And again and in,
He just might get the black.
He's just going to hit and . . .
'Boys time for bed.'
'OK Mum. Come on John.'

Jack Bailey (11)
Maldon Court Preparatory School

Tomorrow

I like sitting
Because I eat
A tiny bit
No one knows
Because I'm a little nit
'I'm in your hair
I give you gyp.'

Henri Skeens (8)
Maldon Court Preparatory School

The Gala

3, 2, 1 go, ooh a fantastic start
For England a really good dive,
Ozzy's doing breaststroke.
Ah what was that?
England did a duck dive
And hit his head on the bottom
And that must really hurt.

Ozzy is now coming up to England
But England is keeping the lead,
Oh wow Ozzy is going really fast.
They are now neck and neck,
No England, Ozzy, England.
They are really close.
When . . . they have to get out of the bath.

Annie Cousins (10)
Maldon Court Preparatory School

Pigs

Pigs in their sty,
Under the night sky
Even though they are lovely and pink,
They usually make a stink.

Some pigs are small,
Where others are quite tall.
They have a big snout,
And they like to run about.

I like pigs a lot,
I'd like one as a pet,
I'd feed it and play with it,
It would be the cleanest pig
You'd ever met.

Elise Oliver (9)
Maldon Court Preparatory School

Morning Mist

As the caterpillar crawls
Sparkling blackberries look like jewels
And shaggy mushrooms grow,
As small waterfalls flow.

As steaming cows stroll past
milking time at last,
I hear the robins call,
The autumn leaves begin to fall.

I walk down the stony track
Now there's no heading back!
My feet crunch along the ground
Now I am going river bound.

Wild ducks fly up in fear,
Because I am quite near.
Circling above me in the sky,
How I wish that I could fly.

Guy Buckle (9)
Maldon Court Preparatory School

Seasons

I think of trees swaying in the breeze.
I love the sound of bumblebees.
The leaves on the trees are turning brown,
The leaves on the trees are falling down.
Now it's winter it's very cold.
Now my sledge is hard to hold.
Now spring is here
We are walking along a pier.
Wow I see the sun appear.

Sam Chaplin (9)
Maldon Court Preparatory School

The Thrill Of A Roller Coaster

When I queue for a roller coaster
I just can't wait
To get through the metal gate.
Start off slow
Then up high
Now a vertical drop from the sky.
Turn around
Upside down
Hands in the air
Wind in my hair
Roller coaster shaking
Seats vibrating
Coaster comes to a stop
Out we hop.
That was thrilling
But now we're chilling.

Jospehine Cooke (9)
Maldon Court Preparatory School

The Fluffy Dog

I found a fluffy dog one day
And said, 'Do you want to play?'
The dog barked, 'Yes,' so off we went
To have some fun that day.
Then I took him to his owner,
Who was very pleased indeed.
He had some food and water and
Cuddles up to sleep.
I went home for my dinner,
I had chicken, chips and peas,
I couldn't wait to go and see
That fluffy dog after tea.

Deanna Haddow (9)
Maldon Court Preparatory School

The Dragon

The dragon is deadly
It blows out fire.
Flaming hot, red and orange.
He has sharp pointy prickles
Right down his back.
The dragon has big, wide wings,
His name is Jack.
He has white sharp teeth
You wouldn't want to touch
Just in case it hurts too much!
At the very end of his long red tail,
Is a green polkadot
A very odd spot!
He has two triangle-shaped ears
And a mouth that smiles.
My friend Jack, I like him miles.

Phoebe Crane (9)
Maldon Court Preparatory School

Fire

It's hot, it's red, yellow and orange.
It will burn your toast
And makes the room nice and warm.
It cooks the dinner and makes milk warm,
But if you leave a candle alight,
Your house might just burn down.
Without fires we can't have fireworks.
Without fire the world would be a cold place,
The sun is a ball of fire.
The sun keeps the world warm.

Leah Byrne (9)
Maldon Court Preparatory School

Diving Contest

Britain is entering the poolside
The Frenchman is saying, 'Bonjour'
The referee is coming in
And it will soon begin

Britain is climbing up the ladder
The French man has started to shudder
The crowd is going wild
Britain dives

He's
    falling
        down
            down
                and then . . .
Splat!
He does a belly flop
He comes out the pool *red*
With a squashed nose

The French is next
Up the ladder he goes
He climbs up halfway
Then decides it is not his day

He slides down the pole
And sits at the edge
He stretches his arms
And slides off the ledge

And the winner is . . . wait
Britain has gone to get changed
And France has . . . *gone!*
No winners this time folks
Bye!

Isabelle Forester-Muir (10)
Maldon Court Preparatory School

Volleyball In The Aviary

Bill starts with the ball,
The crowd squawks with excitement,
Passes the ball to Sam,
The commentator screeches with delight.

The others follow the ball with their eyes,
'Wahoo!' is heard as heads move in different directions,
Many fall off the branch in confusion,
In comes a flying commentary!

The crowd rages as the first point is scored,
Viewers raise their banners.
Bill is on the floor choking on a cracker,
Viewers squawk, 'Polly wants that cracker!'

The spare is passed onto the field,
Sam hits it with all his might,
The door is opened,
But the match is never finished because
All the birds have fled!

James Carter (10)
Maldon Court Preparatory School

The Final Ashes Test

Hoggard comes up for a fast bowl
And it's spinning round faster and faster
It's gonna touch the ground.

Ponting is looking nervous,
He swings his bat round
And . . . misses! It touches the wickets
And he's out!

They swap over and start the game again.
Ponting bowls and what a lovely shot it was,
Back to the game.

Hoggard strikes . . . the bowl it goes flying
Into Mum's new windowpane
Someone's not going to be a happy bunny.

Mum comes zooming out like a missile and . . .
The game's called off
Because they are grounded.

Cameron McGeachy (10)
Maldon Court Preparatory School

Volleyball In The Aviary

Bill starts with the ball,
The crowd squawks with excitement,
He passes the ball to Sam,
The commentator screeches with delight.

The crowd rages as the first point is scored,
Viewers raise their banners,
Bill is on the floor,
Choking on a cracker,
Viewers squawk, 'Polly wants that cracker!'

The other birds
Follow the ball with their eyes,
'Wahoo,' is heard as heads fly,
Many fall off the branch in confusion,
In comes a flying commentary.

The spare is passed onto the field,
Sam hits it with all his might,
The door is opened,
Oh Bill has just been sold.

Ben Phipps (11)
Maldon Court Preparatory School

The Pool Game

The stadium lights go on
The triangle is set
The cues are chalked.

Walder breaks, a red goes down
Next ball, he missed the red
Bailey's turn, the yellow goes down
The second yellow goes down
The third missed the pocket
Just off the cushion.

Walder gets another red down
And a second and a third and a fourth
Walder has only one ball left, the black
He's missed the black completely, foul.

Bailey gets a yellow, another yellow
And a third, can he get his last yellow?
Yes, both people down to the black.

Bailey lines up.
He's about to shoot and . . .
'Boys, time for bed.'
'OK Mum.'
'Come on Tom.'

Thomas Walder (10)
Maldon Court Preparatory School

Diving Contest

Britain is entering the poolside
The Frenchman is saying, 'Bonjour.'
The referee is coming in
And it will soon begin

Britain is climbing up the ladder
The Frenchman has started to shudder
The crowd is going wild
Britain dives, he's falling
And then *splat* . . . now the Frenchman

He climbs up half-way
Decides it's not his day
So he slides down the pole
And sits on the edge
He stretches his arms
And slides off the ledge

And the winner is . . .
Wait
Britain has gone to get changed
And France has . . .
Gone!
No winners this time folks
Bye!

Lucy Richards (10)
Maldon Court Preparatory School

The Match

The whistle blew
The game began
Rooney passed to Beckham.

Beckham had a hard shot at goal
But the 90-year-old granny saved it.
The 92-year-old, Mary got the ball.
Mary chipped the keeper
So the score turned to 1-0 the grannies.

Scholes gets the ball
And passes to Beckham,
Then Beckham chips the ball to Rooney,
Rooney boots the ball in the back of the net.

So the score turns to 1-1.
Three minutes remaining
And the score is 3-2 to England.
Then Fanny gets the ball
And chips the ball to Mary.
Mary passes to the 97-year-old granny
The granny does a bicycle kick
In the top corner.

David Beckham and his teammates
Went shopping, while the old grannies
Got some ice cream.

Luke Saggs (10)
Maldon Court Preparatory School

The Final Ashes Test

Hoggard comes up for a bowl
And it spins round and round.
It's gonna touch the ground.

Ponting is looking nervous
And he swings the bat round
And . . . misses. It touches the wickets
And he's out.

They swap over and start the game.
Ponting bowls, and what a lovely shot it was
Back to the game.

Hoggard strikes the ball
It goes flying into Mum's new windowpane
And Mum rushes out of the kitchen . . .

And the game's stopped because
They are both grounded.

Emily Sach (10)
Maldon Court Preparatory School

The Night Before Christmas

On the night before Christmas
Evil creatures awake for blood
Howls and screams break the silence
And death draws near
The mist thickens, the road becomes thinner
Blood drops and the dead rise
On the night before Christmas no one wakes.

Edward Neal (10)
Montgomery Junior School

The Aquarium

I walk through the aquarium
I feel sacred
I am the only one there
Looking at this blue fantasy
An underwater dimension
I see shimmering fish feeding on anemones
Fish scampering, avoiding sharks
Moonlight flickers from above, spying into their aquatic world
As I see sharks nudging the moonlit surface
I feel a chill as I spot them
They dive down like a flash
And catch their prey
A fish glides down like a feather
It feels almost magical
I sneak closer to the glass
And see more of the underwater life
Anemones shooting under a rock crevice
As an eight-legged creature swims gracefully past
Spraying black ink to the sandy floor
I end my underwater journey
I see the exit ahead
I will dream about this tonight when I go to bed.

Scott Hughes (10)
Montgomery Junior School

My Secret Box

(Based on 'Magic Box' by Kit Wright)

I shall put in my box . . .
A rabbit that is running.
The smell of the breeze outside.
The sound of the sweet birds singing.
Gold, the colour of the rising sun.

Georgia Taylor-Gurney (8)
Montgomery Junior School

The Ghosts

They come out at night
Send a terrifying shiver down your spine
The ghosts will give your doom!
It's a misty winter's night
The ground is covered with frothy thick snow
Trees are bare, their fingers creaking to the wind
Nobody is up, all are sleeping
The graveyard awakes!
All the ghosts rise
Making a deafening screech
But the people do not move
The ghosts glide to the village to cause more misery
Tonight the ghosts pick one house to destroy or make suffer
It's number 23
They sweep through the front door
And sense out the person that will die tonight
Up the stairs they fly, entering the small bedroom
One ghost flies inside the person
Then quickly leaves the room
As the human turns from peach to white
The ghosts exit the house
And go back to their graves
Morning comes
The glistening sun destroys the snow
The people get up
Then a dreaded scream
The police
The hospital
And find out that the victim of house 23
Did not have a heart, but a fossil!

Tamazin Crossman (10)
Montgomery Junior School

My Secret Box

(Based on 'Magic Box' by Kit Wright)

I will put in my box . . .
A snoozing dog on a rug
A miaowing cat
A dog sneezing out loud
Purple because I think it's funny
My friend telling jokes
A cloud of marshmallow for me to float on
A Brussels sprout because it is sweet
And sweets that are chewy
I will put in my box . . .
Roald Dahl books and
Charlie and the Chocolate Factory collectibles
And a yellow bunny that flies
My box is made of snakeskin
And pumice rocks for corners.

Alice Neal (7)
Montgomery Junior School

My Secret Box

(Based on 'Magic Box' by Kit Wright)

I will put in my box . . .
A snoozing dog by the fire
The sound of a car horn
A dancing elephant
A speaking jet plane
My best conkers
My box has stars and moons all over it
It has a duck's beak hinge.

Jessica Ellis (7)
Montgomery Junior School

My Secret Box

(Based on 'Magic Box' by Kit Wright)

I will put in my box . . .
a cat singing cha cha,
a parrot making a cat noise,
the hottest curry in the world,
melting chocolate,
lots and lots of money.
My box is made of gold snowbirds,
claws and the hardest metal in the world.
It is covered with feathers.

Jarrad Bowie (7)
Montgomery Junior School

My Secret Box

(Based on 'Magic Box' by Kit Wright)

I will put in my box . . .
a dog's bark in the morning,
the smell of bacon as I go for a run,
purple and pink,
and a big sorry from my friend.
My box is made of gold.

Karli Allison (7)
Montgomery Junior School

My Secret Box

(Based on 'Magic Box' by Kit Wright)

I will put in my box . . .
a hamster doing monkey bars on the top of his cage
a talking and singing apple rolling downstairs
a kangaroo wrestling in a wrestling match
a dinosaur with sharp claws eating a grain of rice.
My box is made of dog claws and felt.

Aaron Homer (7)
Montgomery Junior School

My Secret Box

(Based on 'Magic Box' by Kit Wright)

I will put in my box . . .
an elephant drinking some water
the sound of the wind blowing
and the colour blue in the rainbow.
I will put in my box . . .
a talking dog.
My box is made of
crystal and the corners
are made of tigers' claws,
pictures of lions cover my box.

Benjamin Logan (7)
Montgomery Junior School

My Secret Box

(Based on 'Magic Box' by Kit Wright)

I will put in my box . . .
a tree trunk
a classroom.

I will put in my box . . .
an elephant that is blue and black
and yellow and orange and green.

I will put in my box . . .
a Tyrannosaurus rex and a black leaf.

My box is made with a leaping spring
and gold and silver crystals.

Callum Kerridge (7)
Montgomery Junior School

Untitled

The bubbles are gently popping,
The colours of the bubbles are
Pink and blue and white.
They're soapy water.

Leah Hurley (7)
St Edward's CE Primary School, Romford

The Ant And The Anteater

(Inspired by 'The Owl and the Pussycat' by Edward Lear)

The ant and the anteater went to Spain
In a beautiful pinky-red van
They took some jam and plenty of spam
And they never went back again.

Heather Nye (7)
St Edward's CE Primary School, Romford

The Ant And The Butterfly

(Inspired by 'The Owl and the Pussycat' by Edward Lear)

The ant and butterfly went to the pub
In a bright yellow, spotty sub,
They took a sharp pencil and a thin stencil
And bumped into a bathtub.

Sarah Brown (9)
St Edward's CE Primary School, Romford

The Owl And The Rat

(Inspired by 'The Owl and the Pussycat' by Edward Lear)

The owl and the rat went to the shops
In a funny one-wheeled car,
To get some mops and silly crops,
They went this way and that - not very far.

Jessica Blake (7) & Lauren Taylor (7)
St Edward's CE Primary School, Romford

Bubbles

Bubbles sink down into the ground
They start up and then go down
They are see-through
Bubbles are good to play with.

Samuel Daly (7)
St Edward's CE Primary School, Romford

The Rat And The Dog

(Inspired by 'The Owl and the Pussycat' by Edward Lear)

The rat and the dog went into town,
In a great pink lorry with spots.
They took some treats and plenty of sweets
And they lost the treats in the knots.

Charlotte Crane (8) & Abigail Diett (7)
St Edward's CE Primary School, Romford

Bubbles

Bubbles are shiny and pretty,
They fly in the wind
And when they fall they pop
And disappear into thin air.

Rebecca Negus (7)
St Edward's CE Primary School, Romford

The Horse And The Dog

(Inspired by 'The Owl and the Pussycat' by Edward Lear)

The horse and the dog went to the circus,
In a funny two-wheeled car.
They took some buns and bubblegum,
But on the way they didn't get far,
In that funny two-wheeled car.

Jed Allen & Olivia Tibbott (7)
St Edward's CE Primary School, Romford

The Blob Or Galaxies Away

I once had a friend called Bob,
He was nothing but a blob.
He always seemed galaxies away,
Even through the month he loved, May,
But he still seemed galaxies away.

George Goldrick (9)
St Edward's CE Primary School, Romford

My Friend, Rachel

F riends are nice and kind
R achel is my friend, my very best friend
I ntroducing herself she is nice and kind
E verything will be fine
N ow we are playing together, we will play all day
D ie tomorrow will meet again.

Aimee Howe (8)
St Edward's CE Primary School, Romford

Fire

F ire can spread, fire can burn, fire's dangerous
I t can hurt so much, you'll regret it
R ighteous people know
E very day a fire.

Karl Gaughran (10)
St Edward's CE Primary School, Romford

Fire

F ire makes me feel like I want to be cross
I see flames burning around me
R apid fire going up then disappearing
E veryone runs in circles screaming.

Samuel Cooke (9)
St Edward's CE Primary School, Romford

Bubbles

Bubbles, bubbles floating into the air
Sinking down on the ground
Very colourful colours
Come down from the sky
If you put them in a balloon you will fly
Up, up into the sky, like a butterfly.

Jessica Lord (7)
St Edward's CE Primary School, Romford

There Was A Man

There was a young man from China
Who thought he was a good climber
He fell off a rock
And off came his socks
And then went to eat at the diner.

Michael Nance (9)
St Edward's CE Primary School, Romford

John Gain

There is a man called John Gain
He is a real pain
He comes from Spain
And he likes to dance in the rain.

Michael Swan (9)
St Edward's CE Primary School, Romford

Dogs

D ogs can bark
O r run fast
G oing wild in the park.

George Swallow (8)
St Edward's CE Primary School, Romford

Volcano

V icious eruptions
O ne after the other
L ava pouring out
C heeping birds fly away
A nd everyone's got away
N ervous people running away
O K.

Hannah Staggs (10)
St Edward's CE Primary School, Romford

Volcano

V olcano, volcano so, so hot
O ver and over it goes
L ower and lower it goes
C areful, careful, be aware
A nd over and lower it goes
N ever, never touch the volcano
O ver and under it goes.

Elizabeth Tran (10)
St Edward's CE Primary School, Romford

Dragons

D ragons are defeating
R apidly meeting
A pparently seating
G oogly greeting
O nce seeking
N oon eating
S ince sleeping
   about treating.

Elena Sheridan (9)
St Edward's CE Primary School, Romford

Earthquake

I heard the ground rumble
I heard the ground shake
I heard my brothers crying
It's an earthquake!
My mum and dad were hiding
My younger brother was whining
My older brother crying
I was trying to think
I hid under the cover
Hoping it was a dream
I heard some people calling
They were calling me to come
I took off the cover
Now look at what I see
I saw the ground ruined
I saw some houses gone
I saw some windows shattered
Look at what it's done.

Tiffany Afoké (10)
St Edward's CE Primary School, Romford

Bubbles

Bubbles floating in the air
and sound of a
gentle pop
they float in
the air with
wonderful
colours.
When
you
blow
them they move all around
with a gentle sound.

Esther Ojo (7)
St Edward's CE Primary School, Romford

Volcano

Volcano, volcano, he's bursting with rage,
He's gonna collapse, quick his face is beige.
He's gushing with anger, please no, no, no!
He's gonna burst like a volcano.
This can't be happening, this can't be true
And no he does not need to go to the loo.
He's pushing and pushing, his face has gone red,
Oh no he might be dead.
He's pushing so hard, now his face is purple,
Oh my god he's chucking up fur balls.
Oh that's it, he's burst into a ball,
Don't worry he's not dead, he's at the hospital.

Beau Lyons (9)
St Edward's CE Primary School, Romford

The Cat In The Hat

The cat in the hat went up to space
In his pink sporty rocket.
He went past all the planets
And collected some blankets
To make them warm.
On the way home
They had some lockets.

Sarah-Jade Stewart (8) & Georgina Every (7)
St Edward's CE Primary School, Romford

The Rabbit With A Habit

There was once a rabbit
Who had such a habit
Of eating Heinz baked beans
That habit made him so mean
And he made a friend called Jean.

Lucy Andrean (9)
St Edward's CE Primary School, Romford

Teacher

Chocolate lover
Weekend lover
Neat work carer
Happy worker
Silence person
Kids lover
Monday hater
Who am I?

A: teacher.

Folasade Cline-Thomas (8)
St Edward's CE Primary School, Romford

Bubbles

Bubbles,
Bubbles, everywhere,
Gently popping in the air.
Floating up,
Floating down,
Floating all around.

Benjamin Paisley (7)
St Edward's CE Primary School, Romford

Bubbles

Gently
moving
through the air,
all sorts of colours.
When you blow them they
soon go *pop!*
It's wonderful to see them
floating through the air,
glistening in
the light.

Laura Johnson (7)
St Edward's CE Primary School, Romford

My Pets

Today I got a puppy
And his name is Riggs
His ears are all floppy
And he likes the name Poppy.

But the day before that
I got a cat and her name is Pat
And right now she's eating a rat.

And I've got a rat called Kat
Kat runs really fast because
Pat chases her round all day long.

And last of all I am getting
A pet better than the rest
I am getting a chinchilla.

But Riggs chases Pat
And Pat chases Kat
And my chinchilla is still left to come.

Jessica Pitts (9)
St Edward's CE Primary School, Romford

Dinosaur

Swift hunter
Extinct killer
Jurassic walker
Scaled terror
Giant destroyer
Fierce carnivore
Terrible lizard
Dead hunter
Destructive giant
Prehistoric reptile
Excellent approacher
Jagged toother
Guess who I am if you dare.

Mez Boateng (8)
St Edward's CE Primary School, Romford

Guinea Pigs

G reat to play with
U seful
I mportant
N ice creatures
E asy to look after
A harmless animal

P oo everywhere
I mpatient
G uinea pigs are lovely
S pecial in every way.

Malanda Cowley (9)
St Edward's CE Primary School, Romford

Swift Mover

Tail rattler
Eye flicker
Teeth spitter
Swift mover
Head wiper
Strong strangler
Skin ripper
Gripping gripper
Wicked climber.

Samuel Gowland (8)
St Edward's CE Primary School, Romford

Sweet Shop

I went into a sweet shop
I saw a giant gobstopper
And when I eventually got it in my mouth
My cheeks went pop, pop, popper.

Corrin Lacey (9)
St Edward's CE Primary School, Romford

The Tree

The tree stood massive and wide,
like a house with branches,
like a rocket on the ground
and he saw fresh green leaves
and long brown branches

He felt frightened
in case he got chopped down,
the others laughed which made him feel useless,
he wanted to run away
and never be seen again

The tree wailed as he heard the sound of chopping,
the tree looked down and then knew why,
he let out one last scream of horror
and then he went down,
you could hear his leaves rustle
in the breeze and on the ground.

Joseph Powell (10)
St Edward's CE Primary School, Romford

Sports

I like to play rounders,
I grip the bat tight,
I also like ice skating,
Jumping and gliding in blue boots.

With a bat and a ball,
I play tennis,
Over here, over there, everywhere,
I always lose.

With a kick of a ball
I play football,
I run here and there
And then *I score!*

Katherine Miller (9)
St Edward's CE Primary School, Romford

The Tree

The tree smiled happily
Early one spring morning
He looked down and saw the pretty buds
Which were dancing in the sun
He noticed some little children
Playing a game of hide-and-seek.

The tree closed his eyes
And suddenly he felt a hand
Then he felt another
He opened his eyes and frowned
One of the playmates was climbing him
The tree smiled and laughed.

The little friends soon left him
All of a sudden he felt alone
He could hear the tiny children
Skipping in the leaves and chuckling
The voices started to fade
As they ran away with joy.

Rhiannon Townson (10)
St Edward's CE Primary School, Romford

Friendship

F or a really good reason
R ound and round
I n and out of houses
E ndless fun
N o one falls out of a lovely friendship
D ilemmas are solved by one another
S ounding great with a grateful mate
H as a lot of sleepovers with a lot of sweets
I ntelligence does not matter
P ounding on the bad and singing with the good.

Sophie Hughes (9)
St Edward's CE Primary School, Romford

Babies

Babies like to poop
Their nappies always droop
Why are they so small?
Some even think they're cool!
Crying all the time
It should be made a crime
Sucking their dummies
Getting bigger tummies
Caleb's sister can fight
Ouch! That gives me a fright
When they grow up they're alright
As long as they don't bite
They can get chickenpox
They look like little dots
Wow, they're mad!

Joel Oyelese (9)
St Edward's CE Primary School, Romford

My Fears

Baby ants topple,
Jellyfish wobble,
Spiders in houses,
Cat pounces on mouses,
Pythons up trees,
Millions of bees,
Lions roar loudly,
Ducks like it cloudy,
Tigers are stripy,
Hedgehogs are spiky,
Monkeys like trees,
But have thousands of fleas,
They made me have tears,
These are all of my fears.

Phoebe Leung (9)
St Edward's CE Primary School, Romford

Moonlight

The moonlight can see you,
You can see it.
At night it shines at you,
It shines on me.
The moonlight can see the whole world
And everyone on it.

You can feel it,
The moonlight can feel you
Only if you go on a rocket into space
In your dreams,
You think you can live on it
And feel it every day.

You can't hear it,
It can hear you
Snoring all night long.

Daniel Haynes (10)
St Edward's CE Primary School, Romford

Best Friends

B est friends are
E xcellent
S tars
T alented

F riendly
R ecently
I maginitive
E ver so
N ice
D ecent and
S pecial.

Modupe Olagundoye (9)
St Edward's CE Primary School, Romford

In the Playground

What I can see . . .

I can see the children playing on the slides,
laughing like they're being wise,
having lots of fun in the sunshine glum.
That's the end of my poem, I hope you liked it,
So see you later alligator and don't forget I'll be here later.

What I can hear . . .

I can hear the children shouting,
I can hear the bouncy castle going down,
I can hear people scoring goals,
I can hear the children laughing in the sun.

What I can feel and smell . . .

I can feel the atmosphere going wild,
I can feel the children rushing through the wind,
I can smell the packed lunches smelling like the whole of KFC.

Courtney Howell (10)
St Edward's CE Primary School, Romford

Teachers

If you look in the lounge
The teachers are always there
Sitting and ignoring us
They don't even care!

The teachers are always smoking!
Really it stinks!
And if you look at Mr Jones
He's always pouring drinks!

When we went on a school trip
When we touched the deer
But by the time we got back home
The teachers were drinking beer.

Lauren Angus-Larkin (9)
St Edward's CE Primary School, Romford

The Moonlight

The moonlight is surrounded by beautiful stars
The moonlight looked down and saw lit up buildings
Beside he saw a row of multicoloured cars.

The moonlight threw the light over the forest
He saw a thousand animals
That looked like a big army.

The moonlight felt lonely
He had no one to speak to
All he did was look down
He heard happiness all around.

Kenneth Omole (10)
St Edward's CE Primary School, Romford

The Sparkly Moonlight

The glowing moonlight looked down at the
Beautifully coloured Earth as he was singing
Watching the stars sparkle in the dark blue sky.
As the moonlight swirled round, the air touched his face
Whilst he was singing to the sun as it was rising.
The moonlight could hear the air whistling peacefully
As the air swirled and twirled and danced around.

Kearney Mott (11)
St Edward's CE Primary School, Romford

Space Monkey 6000

Space monkey went to a planet.
He saw a rabbit and its habit was eating carrots.
He went down and didn't make a frown
And it was an amazing town, they got him a crown.
It went down the toilet, so he flushed himself down.

Regan Mott (9)
St Edward's CE Primary School, Romford

My Toys

I love my toys
I've got . . .
A monkey, a lion
A cat, a dog
A fish, a guinea pig
A bear and
All together they
Make my bed
I love my toys.

Alexandra Wood (9)
St Edward's CE Primary School, Romford

My Teacher

My teacher is helpful,
My teacher is kind,
My teacher is ever so pretty.

My teacher is wicked,
My teacher is great,
Oh my teacher is ever so funny.

My teacher likes rabbits,
My teacher likes blue,
My teacher is just the best.

Siân West (9)
St Edward's CE Primary School, Romford

There Was A Young Man

There was a young man called Bob
Who wanted to get a job.
He looked in the pages,
For ages and ages
And then he began to sob.

Rowan Barnes (9)
St Edward's CE Primary School, Romford

A Stampede Of Bulls!

The sea marched to the shore
In an angry rage
Knocking everything in his path
Shouting angry, nasty protests
Like a stampede of bulls!

The sea was unpopular
The sea ran away
The sea was unhappy
Though his friends could assure
That the people of the town
Were just angry and worried
Of being grabbed by a mysterious hand!

The sea came back
You could hear the cheers
From miles around
They were sad when he had been gone
There was a lack of gladness
But now they were cheering
Like a stampede of bulls!

Anthony Wise (10)
St Edward's CE Primary School, Romford

The Raging River!

You can see the raging river,
You can see the roaring river,
Like a bear in the dark forest.

You can feel the calm water passing,
You can feel the calm water flowing by,
Like a bird singing softly.

You can hear the water swishing,
You can hear the water swashing,
Near the river bank.

Bethaney Hall (10)
St Edward's CE Primary School, Romford

The Forest

I can see:
the trees swaying gently
with their branches waving at me
the beautiful birds flying swiftly from tree to tree
a scary hunter with a gun.

I can hear:
the banging of the gun
the wailing of the animals
and the rustling of the noisy bushes

I can feel:
a monkey on my head
the heat of a fire
and the water rushing through my toes

I can smell:
the forest fire
the animals' droppings
and my dinner.

Abigail Howson (10)
St Edward's CE Primary School, Romford

The Deep Dark Forest

The deep dark forest,
Roared in horror
At the sight of a lonely traveller.

The deep dark forest
Felt in pain,
As it was weakening.

The deep dark forest
Heard a yell of dismay
As it was walking through the swaying branches.

Lauren Kaufman (10)
St Edward's CE Primary School, Romford

The Magical Rainforest

What I can see:

I can see the glistening river flowing,
Spitting rain splatting on the floor,
The monkeys, swinging through the trees,
The staring jaguar watching me.

What I can hear:

I can hear the rushing river,
The howling monkeys in the trees,
The hissing snakes at my feet,
Snapping crocodiles in the lake.

What I can smell and feel:

I can smell the fruit on the trees,
Tingling fish swimming through my toes,
The smell of the tribes burning fire,
The dripping, dropping rain on my hands.

What I can taste:

I can taste the wonderful huge berries,
The cool breeze in my mouth,
The refreshing rain on my teeth,
The tribe's food burning on the fire.

Claire Jackson (10)
St Edward's CE Primary School, Romford

The Sea

The sea is a cup of tea as flat as can be.
The sea is soft and fluffy and light blue.

Reaching with its soft bubbly hands
Trying to stretch and tickle your toes.

The sea whistled gently as it came to shore
Saying, 'I am a calm shore.'

Jade Hearn (10)
St Edward's CE Primary School, Romford

The Rainforest

I can see the beautiful rainforest,
With trees and bushes, with fruits and berries.
All the animals and coloured birds,
The massive lake with huge crocodiles and there's a river.

I can hear the wonderful singing birds,
The snapping crocodiles and the laughing monkeys.,
The leaves rustling in the trees
And the rushing river, the soft refreshing rain,
Dropping on the ground.

I can feel the soft rain and the leaves from the tree on my head.
I feel calm, excited being here,
I also feel relaxed.

I can smell the different coloured flowers
And the delicious fruit from the trees.
I can smell the animals
And my packed lunch in my back pack.

Rachel Stewart (10)
St Edward's CE Primary School, Romford

The Tree

The tree looked at a flower,
Opening in the new spring air,
Later, he saw a boy picking
That flower for his mother.

The tree felt happy when he saw children,
Playing on the wet, green grass.
He felt comforted when children sat on him,
Holding him ever so tightly.

At night he heard scary noises,
Lurking on other trees.
The tree heard frightening noises.
But he soon went to sleep.

Thomas Harvey (10)
St Edward's CE Primary School, Romford

The Sea

The sea opened his eyes
To see all the children
Playing in his wavy waves

The sea felt very angry
So he ran to the shore
And grabbed everything on the sandy beach

The sea woke up to the sound
Of thunder and lightning
So he joined with roaring.

Elsie Lawrence (10)
St Edward's CE Primary School, Romford

The Stream

The stream looked up to the sky,
It saw the birds go by,
Saw the sun brighter than ever.

The stream felt the vibration go through it,
It felt the giant salmon swim around it.

The stream heard the deer rush by,
The stream heard the trees fall asleep.

Liam Wheeler (10)
St Edward's CE Primary School, Romford

Mountain

I can glance at the bright white glaciers
That tumble down my side

I can feel the freezing cold frost
That tingles on my body

I can listen to the ear exploding noise
Where gigantic lumps of ice have marched down too far.

Thomas Greene (10)
St Edward's CE Primary School, Romford

The Forest

The forest opened its eyes
It saw the beautiful churning waves
It spoke to them as it saw
The misty cloud in the sky.

The forest heard
The traveller tumbling
The forest marched
Down and down to save him.

The forest felt
That everyone was dull and boring
So he sung them a song
To cheer them up.

Charlotte Tibbott (10)
St Edward's CE Primary School, Romford

The Sky

The shining sky can see everything in his path
With his bright blue eyes
And can feel the sun as he sunbathes
And can hear the roaring cars pass by.

The twinkling sky saw his friends
As they walked by,
Could feel himself worrying,
As they did not say goodbye.

The swarming sky saw his destiny
And fainted as it was the love of his life.
He felt worried
As he heard her say goodnight.

Arabella Weymouth (10)
St Edward's CE Primary School, Romford

Rainforest Magic

What I can see:

Multicoloured birds soaring through the air
Trees waving in the distance as friendly as my best friend
Optimistic baby orang-utans falling from the trees
But always finding fruit
The gleaming river glistening in the sunshine too

What I can hear:

The river's waves rushing by
Beats of the tribe's home-made drums
Children's cackles flowing through the air
Parrots and monkeys chattering
And tiny birds tweeting
Alligators and crocodiles snapping fiercely in the swamps

What I can feel and smell:

I can feel a mixture of comfort and fear
The Amazon is as relaxing as a massage room
The tribal people live in happiness
I can feel the twigs crunch beneath my feet
The smell of tribal food fill the air
I can feel the gentle raindrops and the breeze.

Elizabeth McDonald (10)
St Edward's CE Primary School, Romford

Winter's Here

Summer falls, winter's here
The snow that slashes on the ground
Stuck inside bored and cold
All around there's no sound.

Jessica-Rose Spong (9)
St Edward's CE Primary School, Romford

The Playground

I can see children crying and screaming for their mothers.
I can see people sliding down the towering slide.
I can see children shouting higher to their parents on the swings.
I can see children like monkeys on the monkey bars.

I can hear people singing, 'I'm the king of the castle
And you're the dirty rascal,' from the top of the climbing frame.
I can hear boys laughing on the swings.
I can hear girls showing off on the slide.

I can feel the excited children pushing to get to the swings.
I can feel the rain falling on the children's heads.
I can feel the excitement in all the little children
And I can smell ice cream.

Daisy Harper (10)
St Edward's CE Primary School, Romford

The Rainforest

What I can see is the green, green grass,
The swaying trees waving at me,
The cheetahs chatting to each other,
The flowers waking up from their long deep sleep.

What I can hear is birds' voices singing joyfully,
The wild waterfall beating down on the water below,
A lion being as noisy as a screaming child,
Crunching crackling leaves under my feet.

What I can feel and smell is the fresh free air,
The meat that the roaring lion ate,
The gentle rushing rain,
The sticky sap on my hands.

Rianna Veares (10)
St Edward's CE Primary School, Romford

Raining Forest

What I can see:

Long slithering snakes, sliding across the muddy path.
Three hungry alligators in the swamp.
Trees surrounding me, 'Look there's a bird.'
I can see small, cheeky monkeys throwing coconuts at each other.
Bees getting their pollen.

What I can hear:

I can hear birds tooting, monkeys howling.
Chimps chatting, rain splatting, tigers growling.
Snakes hissing, alligators snapping.
Flying frogs jumping from tree to tree.

What I can smell:

I can smell the fresh rain dripping to the ground.
I looked around and saw a leopard looking at me.
I didn't want to see that it was licking its lips.
I ran for my life!

I can feel:

I can feel the fear bubbling in my heart.
I tripped over a stone and fell to the ground with a big thump.
The leopard caught me up, my heart stopped.
I could feel the pain in my knee
But with one big gulp the leopard ate me

And that was the end of me!

Elise Herring (10)
St Edward's CE Primary School, Romford

The Wardrobe Monster

There's a monster in my wardrobe at night,
he gives me a great, great fright.
There's a ghost in my garden at night,
who gives me a bright, bright light.

Charlie Turner (8)
St Edward's CE Primary School, Romford

There's A . . .

There's a ghost in my TV
At night
He gives me a big, big fright
He was trapped there
Years ago
And he's lost his giant toe
There's a ghost
In my bedroom
At night
He gives me
A huge, huge fright
He was trapped there
Years ago
And he's lost his
Middle toe
There's a ghost in my garden
At night
He gives me a garden
Great, great fright
He was trapped there years ago
And he's lost his little toe.

Lynden Reed (8)
St Edward's CE Primary School, Romford

Moonlight

The moonlight stared around the town,
looking for his old mate the sun,
but he did not know where his friend had gone.

He was bored waiting for his friend,
looking tired and weary all day long
and wishing his friend would turn up.

Then he heard his friend calling his name,
Moon, where are you, where are you?
He saw his friend smiling at him.

Joshua Barnes (10)
St Edward's CE Primary School, Romford

My Favourite Animal Is A?

Fast runner
Spot lover
Meat eater
Tree climber
Jungle dweller
Leaf hater
Good spyer
Wide eyer
Game winner
Effort giver
Best chaser
Flesh ripper
Liver liker
Four legger
Small header.
What is it?

A: A cheetah.

Axton Reed (8)
St Edward's CE Primary School, Romford

Down In The Rainforest

I can see the spectacularly, sweetly singing birds,
The cheeky chattering toucans,
The tall and stately trees
Gently swaying in the breeze.
I can see the croaking frogs
And the large fleshy fruits
And the birds doing their beautiful little toots,
Lakes overflowing,
But, no, I'm not going.
I can see the insects jumping,
The leaves are gently dumping
The rain onto the ground.

Hannah Lauder (11)
St Edward's CE Primary School, Romford

The Forest

What I can see:

A large tall tree
With smooth brown and yellow bark.
The soft red, yellow and brown leaves,
Falling down to the ground.
The silky water running through the lake.

What I can hear:

The gentle winds softly rushing in my face.
The tree swaying slightly.
People treading softly in all the leaves.
The trickling of the river
And splashes of the pool and the waterfall.

What I can feel and smell:

I can feel icy cold refreshing water,
The summer rain falling softly on my head.
I can smell the fleshy and smooth fruits
Dangling on the tall tree
And that is the forest.

Cecily Henman (11)
St Edward's CE Primary School, Romford

The Moonlight

Can you see the moonlight, travelling through the sky?
Can you see the moonlight, jumping over the forest?
Can you see the moonlight, dancing with the stars?

Can you feel the moonlight, rubbing against your head?
Can you feel the moonlight, tickling your feet?
Can you feel the moonlight, shining over you?

Can you hear the moonlight, fighting with the sun?
Can you hear the moonlight, laughing with the forest?
Can you hear the moonlight, saying farewell?
And with a sigh, he went because morning was coming.

Henry Eades (10)
St Edward's CE Primary School, Romford

The Tall Tree

The tree watched the water
Jumping up and down
He saw his neighbour

The water made him feel calm
He felt jolly next to his neighbour
Together in the forest

The tree could hear the birds sing
They sang jolly songs
He heard the fish swimming by, in the rushing water.

William Fenton (10)
St Edward's CE Primary School, Romford

Sharks

Sharks are big, sharks are small,
Sharks are naughty, sharks are bad.
A great white is very deadly,
Are sharks bad? We do not know.
So sharks are very vicious.
Snap, snap, bite, bite,
You don't want to meet a great white.

Luke McClenaghan (8)
St Edward's CE Primary School, Romford

Trees

Stare like a lion at its prey
as the river jumps the jagged rocks.

The birds gently rest in their nest
like lions do, waiting for nightfall.

Whistle quietly like a mouse
through the dancing branches.

Joshua Dunning (10)
St Edward's CE Primary School, Romford

Colchester Zoo

C ats miaow
O tters swim
L eopards run
C ats are fun
H owling dog
E very hog
S it beside the frog
T igers roar
E mus are for
R unning really fast

Z ebras kick
O tters swim
O ctopuses stick.

Lily Sharpe (8)
St Edward's CE Primary School, Romford

Rainforest

Monkeys all around me, big and small,
Trees all around me, large and tall,
Frogs all around me, big and fat,
Rain falling softly upon my hat.

Birds singing peacefully,
Rivers rushing gracefully,
Some leaves swaying lazily,
Some leaves swaying crazily.

I smell berries here and there,
On some trees I smell a pear.
I feel excited,
I feel delighted.

Tom Read (10)
St Edward's CE Primary School, Romford

Animals

D olphins are kind
O ctopuses are cool and have eight legs
L eopards are fast, cool and mean
P andas are sweet and nice to meet
H issing snakes are vicious and cruel
I cy penguins in the sea
N esting birds in the tree
S harks in the sea cool and mean
    But most of all I like dolphins.

Rachel Phelan (8)
St Edward's CE Primary School, Romford

My Pet

I wonder what the choice would be
If the choice was up to me.
Would it be something small and hairy
Or something tall and very scary?
Would it be something wide and fat
Or something short just like a cat,
Or would it be a creature with a horn
Just like a unicorn?

Harriet Blowers (8)
St Edward's CE Primary School, Romford

Holidays

H ome (don't want to be there)
O range (is very nice)
L ovely (want to stay)
I ce (in my drink)
D uvet (comfortable and cosy)
A nts (not that many around)
Y ummy (fruit everywhere).

Rosie Jennings (8)
St Edward's CE Primary School, Romford

All Weather

The sun is hot
The wind is breezy
The snow is freezing
So I get cold.
I love the leaves
When they fall off trees
Then they stay there in a heap.
I like the flowers
In the spring
Red, white and pink.
I like the winter
In the night
Because we have
A snowball fight.
The summer is fun
In the day,
Because we have
A water fight.

Georgina Allen (9)
St Edward's CE Primary School, Romford

Pop Star Show

I can see all around me, the stage
And all the people, the instruments and my microphone.
I'm nervous but I should be used to it by now.

I can hear the crowd roaring like a lion
And the faint giggles of the girls backstage.
I'm nervous but I should be used to it by now.

I can feel the heat of this boiling room,
Excitement of the people and I can feel
The vibrations of the electric guitars that are warming up.
I feel nervous but I should be used to it by now . . .
I'm famous, everyone loves me!

Katie Butler (11)
St Edward's CE Primary School, Romford

The Luscious Rainforest

What can I see?

Bushes have surrounded me,
Oh look there's a nest up in the tree!
There are brave beautiful birds flying up to the river,
Oh no, I just saw something slither!

What can I hear?

The wind is whispering to the trees
Dropping on the forest's ferny floor are beautiful leaves.
Prowling tigers and slithering snakes
Are coming towards me, like big thin rakes!

What can I smell?

I can smell the fruit on the trees
The flowers with their pretty leaves,
The freshness of the rain
And rotting bark that seems to be in pain!

What can I feel?

I feel so fresh
But oh no, I feel the snake after my flesh!
Fear is rising up inside me!
I don't care about the mosquitoes that will bite me!

I hope that's not the end of me!

Emma Cottrell (10)
St Edward's CE Primary School, Romford

Lost Not Found

If you ever drink cold water,
You'll end up in hot Malta,
If you give your dog a bone,
It'll end up like a stone
And it'll never be found again.

Hope Joanne Garnish (9)
St Edward's CE Primary School, Romford

Dazzling Dancers Of The Night

I could hear a full audience of people,
clapping and cheering,
I could hear them calling, 'Well done,
you did great, you did well.'
But most of all I wish, I wish my parents
could be there.

I could see many smiles, so many,
many happy faces.
I could see costumes of different shapes
and sizes,
with glitter all around.
Men wore smart bow ties and suits of black,
white and navy.

I could feel my feet drowning in my soft,
velvet shoes.
I could feel the buttons and laces on my dress
getting tighter and tighter,
as the dark, starry night swept over our heads
the show began to end.
When the curtains dropped, I could feel my heart
thumping away like mad,
but most of all I wish, I wish my parents
could be there.

Faye Martin (10)
St Edward's CE Primary School, Romford

I Love Animals

I can swing on a tree like a monkey.
I can swim like a dolphin in the sea.
And starfish sing like little animals,
And best of all, I love animals sweet
Because they are cute and silky and fluffy
And shiny, shaped like a star.

Zoe Corbin (8)
St Edward's CE Primary School, Romford

A Soldier In War

People lying on the floor in agony
and bullets flying past my head
and massive explosions.

Fires, the planes above me and
people screaming in pain.

The bullets bouncing on my helmet
and my heavy machine gun
and when I fire it, it comes back at me
twice as fast.

Smoke from the bombs and blood
from the floor, bodies lying lifeless
and still no more!

Oliver Haynes (10)
St Edward's CE Primary School, Romford

Great White Shark

A great white is known for its size,
A great white is dangerous to us.
A great white's teeth rip its prey in half,
A great white can fight like a bear,
You don't want to meet a great white shark
Or you'll be its meal.

Aiden Jackson (8)
St Edward's CE Primary School, Romford

Untitled

(Inspired by 'The Owl and the Pussycat' by Edward Lear)

The horse and the kitten went to Disneyland
In a pink and purple spotty plane.
They had some fun and ate some buns
While in the plane going to Spain.

Rebecca Staggs (8) & Grace Pawley (7)
St Edward's CE Primary School, Romford

The Highwayman

I can see the golden, shining rich man's cart
coming towards me.

I can hear the galloping of a heavy horse
and the shot from a rifle.

I can feel the sharp stabbing pain
in my brown left leg where I got shot.
The pain was unbearable.

I can taste the tongue-turning taste
of cold oozing blood that I'm bringing up
along with saliva.

I can smell the terrible smell of fear,
and the cold red queasy looking blood.

Kelvin Rushbrook (10)
St Edward's CE Primary School, Romford

The Kitten And The Dog
(Inspired by 'The Owl and the Pussycat' by Edward Lear)

The kitten and the dog went to Mercury
In a big smelly sock
They took some food, the kitten was cool
And turned into a dude with a clock.

Bradwell John (7)
St Edward's CE Primary School, Romford

Untitled
(Inspired by 'The Owl and the Pussycat' by Edward Lear)

The owl and the pussycat went to Mars
In a lovely blue and purple spotty boat
The blue gloomy boat was cool
They took some honey and plenty of floats.

Jodi Whitehead & Palvy Manduakila (7)
St Edward's CE Primary School, Romford

The Spiky One

Ant eater
Spiky body
Sand crawler
Ball roller
Enemy defence
Lays eggs
Six inches long
Small reptile
Dessert runner

A: thorny devil.

Dominic Phillips (8)
St Edward's CE Primary School, Romford

Sam The Spider

Sam the spider
Has eight stretchy legs
He bites you
And spikes you
And kicks your legs
He doesn't like humans
He doesn't like birds
That is Sam the spider.

Samuel Kelly (9)
St Edward's CE Primary School, Romford

Rainbow

Red is like a rose
Yellow is like the sun as it glows
Green is as royal as a queen
Orange is fruit that is a sweet
Purple sweets that I like to eat
Blue is all around.

Courtney Morton (8)
St Edward's CE Primary School, Romford

Swan

Bread eater
Duck kisser
Deep thinker
Rain lover
White feathers
Tear stopper
Beautiful white animal
Playing lover
Fish seeker
Girl liker
Boy hater
Fish hater.

Sophie O'Neal (8)
St Edward's CE Primary School, Romford

Chomp, Crunch, Help

Bone cruncher
Big teeth!
Sneaky grin
Flesh chewer
Big muscles
Very large
Bone cracker
Human killer.

Thomas James Butler (8)
St Edward's CE Primary School, Romford

The Piggy And The Picachu

(Inspired by 'The Owl and the Pussycat' by Edward Lear)

The piggy and the picachu went to Florida
Then they went on a red and blue aeroplane
They took a bike, a bath and a steak
They ate and drowned in the bath.

George Wright (9)
St Edward's CE Primary School, Romford

Night-Time Creature

My teeth are like razors
I live on land
I come out at night
I let out a terrifying howl
I attack humans when they're close
I love eating meat
I'm a horrifying pet
I'm as wild as can be.

Emily Shepherd (8)
St Edward's CE Primary School, Romford

Bad Little Boy

Window smasher
Spider killer
Fist breaker
Teacher hater
Bad temper
Homework hater
No friends
Heavy muscles
Bad loser.

Philip Hawkins (8)
St Edward's CE Primary School, Romford

My Boggle

Bedtime cover
Big eyes
Friend lover
Soft tail
Best flyer
Loving carer
Shy forever.

Libby Dejoodt (8)
St Edward's CE Primary School, Romford

Wimbledon

The yellow tennis ball is coming straight towards me,
I'm here, Wimbledon at last, the green grass, the big crowd.
All clapping and shouting, umpires calling the score, the stadium
So big, the opponent, the top 30 in the world.

I can hear the claps, the umpires calling the score and calling
'Balls in' and 'balls out'.

I can feel the racquet grip so smooth, the tennis ball all fluffy,
I can feel the crunch as I walk on the grass, crunch! Crunch!

I smell the green grass, I love that smell, the sweat on my brow
From all that running around, 'Hooray, I've won!'

Robert Lewis (10)
St Edward's CE Primary School, Romford

Dolphins

D olphins are nice, dolphins are kind
O n the day I saw them they were blue and funny,
L ook, I guess you've noticed that dolphins are my best animals.
P eople say that they can be scary but they're not,
H ey guess what? Dolphins are lovely animals.
 I f you ever met them, I bet they would jump up and say, 'Hi'
N ow it's time to say, 'Bye.'

Stephanie Janet Hayden (8)
St Edward's CE Primary School, Romford

Untitled

(Inspired by 'The Owl and the Pussycat' by Edward Lear)

The cat and the rat went to the fair
They went in a mini fast Ferrari
And while they were there
They had to share and sat on a giant pear.

Lois Akinola, Elizabeth Cottrell & Emily Pettitt (7)
St Edward's CE Primary School, Romford

Dancing

There was a dancer who was asked to do a show,
'OK,' she said, 'I'll prepare to go.'
She practised and practised, until she could practise no more,
When she got there, she was surprised at what she saw,
People prancing, people dancing, it was to her galore,
She was wearing a sparkling dress,
For now it was at her possess.

Chop, chop a man made her jump,
She fell on the floor with a bump,
'You're the star of the show,
Get out there and go.'
Her twirl was like a shining pearl,
'I feel like a burning sun
And I'm having so much fun.'

She cried when she had to go,
'Go, go, I can't go now,'
'Don't worry we'll have a show next week,
Come along and take a peep.'

Louise Frost (10)
St Edward's CE Primary School, Romford

Avalanche!

I can see the 'Giant Killer' hurtling itself at me
waiting to kill me, how fast it moves, the white killer.

I can hear the roar of the beast,
I can hear its warning cry,
I also hear its stamping feet.

I can feel the stamping of its feet
as it hurtles down the hill,
I can feel its voice,
shaking the ground getting nearer and nearer
until it strikes me down.

Crash! Crash! Crash!

Sam Walden (10)
St Edward's CE Primary School, Romford

A Bully

Fist fighter
Karate chopper
Heart breaker
Bad temper
Violence maker
Name caller
Rule breaker
Rough toucher
Sick neighbour
My worst enemy.

Hanaa Sakhare (8)
St Edward's CE Primary School, Romford

Pupil

Loud screamer
Playtime lover

Spelling hater
Animal lover

Money bringer
Lunch lover

That's a pupil!

Matthew Lloyd (8)
St Edward's CE Primary School, Romford

Cat And Dog

(Inspired by 'The Owl and the Pussycat' by Edward Lear)

A cat and a dog went to see their friend Frog
On a great big long log.
They took some money and some honey
Because he had a wife frog.

Lynsey Marsden (7)
St Edward's CE Primary School, Romford

Shark

Fish Eater
Water breather
Shark fighter
Man killer
Deep swimmer
Boat finder
Ship follower
Sharp snapper
Rubbish lover.

A: shark.

Jessica Chesney (8)
St Edward's CE Primary School, Romford

Aliens

Aliens are ugly,
Aliens have three eyes.
Aliens are green,
Aliens are liars.
Aliens hate people.
Aliens don't wear cloaks.
Aliens laugh at folks!

Charles Fancourt (8)
St Edward's CE Primary School, Romford

Bubbles

Bubbles nice and bright
Float in the air
They're like a rainbow
We blow bubbles
When we are allowed to pop them
I go at speed
I can see glistening when it is back.

Georgina Rainbird (7)
St Edward's CE Primary School, Romford

Sharks

Sharks are big,
Sharks are small.
Some are very, very cruel,
Sharks can smell a drop of blood
In an Olympic pool.
Some have a good sense of smell,
Some have no sense at all.
Some are very very cool,
That is the end of my poem.

Dami Omotosho (8)
St Edward's CE Primary School, Romford

Special Animal

Meat eater
Fast runner
Long jumper
Tree climber
Neck breaker
Big eater.

I am a cheetah.

Toni Afoke (8)
St Edward's CE Primary School, Romford

The Dog And The Cat
(Inspired by 'The Owl and the Pussycat' by Edward Lear)

The dog and the cat went to Mars
In a funny shaped boat.
They dropped back into the sea
And dropped back into the sea
And had some tea,
Then wore a fluffy coat.

Folakemi Cline-Thomas (7)
St Edward's CE Primary School, Romford

Pets

Cats are cute
Some are big, others are small
A few are lazy, most like to crawl.

Dogs are scary
Most are big, little are small,
Little lazy most like to play.

Rabbits are lovely,
Most are fat, little are thin.
They love carrots,
I don't.

So that's my pet's, farewell!

Holly Peck (8)
St Edward's CE Primary School, Romford

The Horse And The Crocodile

(Inspired by 'The Owl and the Pussycat' by Edward Lear)

The horse and the crocodile went to the beach
They took some slugs in some mud
They went on a boat
But it didn't float
So they fell to the bottom with a thud.

Joseph Bell (8)
St Edward's CE Primary School, Romford

The Cat And Rabbit

(Inspired by 'The Owl and the Pussycat' by Edward Lear)

A cat and a rabbit went to the shops
in a beautiful yellow car.
They took a frock and two socks
and a beautiful top.

Grace Martin (7)
St Edward's CE Primary School, Romford

Animals

A pplauding antelopes combing their hair
B urping baboons asleep in their lair
C hirping cats wailing all night
D ancing dolphins given a fright
E normous elephants stomping around
F erocious fish jump at the sound
G alloping goat, a noisy thing
H umming hare, humming a hymn
I nsulting iguana, insulting like he does
J azzie jaguar wanting a fudge
K iddie kangaroo jumping up and down
L oving lizard going round
M ini monkey, jumping around
N oisy gnats making a horrible sound
O ozing octopus falling asleep
P urring panther playing all day
Q uacking quails having a play
R elaxing rabbit laying down
S lithering snakes frown
T ickling tigers having a fun time
U ttering unicorn writing a rhyme
V ile vulture flying in the air
W ater walrus wet and bare
X -raying X-ray singing a song
Y apping yak going on and on
Z apping zebra having fun in the zoo.

Beth Lamb (8)
St Edward's CE Primary School, Romford

Bubbles

Bubbles float in the air
And come down to gently pop
Shining rainbow colours in the bubble
So pretty, so good.

Yasmin Morris (7)
St Edward's CE Primary School, Romford

In My Body

A pple just been digested
B lood running through the veins
C auliflower being chewed
D isco in the belly
E yeball all fat
F ungus on the brain
G iant brain
H eat pumping the blood
I ndigestive system
J uice from the brain
K idney all fat
L ungs are pumping
M outh with rotten teeth
N ostrils with bogies
O rgans with lots of blood
P ears I've just eaten
Q uavers crackling
R ibs all slimy
S enses smelling rotten
T ongue all wet
U gly guts
V ocal lungs singing
W ater waving down
X ylophone in the bottom
Y ucky earwax
Z oo in your belly.

Tom Maher (8)
St Edward's CE Primary School, Romford

Bubbles

Bubbles, bubbles, bubbles
Beautiful bubbles
They shine so high, they reflect in the sky
Bubbles, bubbles, bubbles.

Feyijimi Tunde (7)
St Edward's CE Primary School, Romford

Great White Shark

A great white shark is known for its size,
Its teeth are pearly and white,
They rip through the victim, like knives.
A great white is dangerous and known for its killing of us.
A great white is ferocious and rips up everything in its path,
It swims through the water like nothing you have ever seen before,
It swims as fast as a cheetah on land.
It fights like a bear,
This is why you never want to come across a great white shark.

Jake Farmer (8)
St Edward's CE Primary School, Romford

Volcano

Terrified, that's what I am
Oversleep, that's what I do
Run, get out of here, that's what I'm going to do
I'm as naughty as you are to me
I am as ready, dump me, I can blow
I am over there, I am over here
I can be everywhere
I am a volcano big and round
Do not make a sound, nobody knows I just might blow.

Foyin Oladapo (9)
St Edward's CE Primary School, Romford

The Horse And The Cow
(Inspired by 'The Owl and the Pussycat' by Edward Lear)

The horse and the cow went to town
In a big lorry full of mud
They took some honey and plenty of money
Which they mixed in a huge round bathtub.

Adam Thain (7)
St Edward's CE Primary School, Romford

Kids

Kids are small, kids are big,
Kids are everywhere, watching the jig.
Kids are boys, kids are girls,
Twists, turns, jumps and curls.
Kids have blond hair, kids have brown,
Sometimes kids make such a howl!
Kids like to run, jump and leap,
But sometimes they accidentally end up in a heap!
Kids like fruit, kids like veg,
Kids like hiding in the hedge!
Kids can shout, kids can play,
Kids like playing in the hay,
And that's the end of our lovely day!

Megan Togwell (8)
St Edward's CE Primary School, Romford

Flood

F orests sinking
L ike everything's disappearing
O h no!
O kay, is the opposite of what people are feeling
D rowning people.

James Gill (9)
St Edward's CE Primary School, Romford

The Cat And The Hamster

(Inspired by 'The Owl and the Pussycat' by Edward Lear)

The cat and the hamster went to the park
on a pink and yellow aeroplane.
They took some fish, they put out a dish
and then dropped them down a big drain.

Christine Ford (7)
St Edward's CE Primary School, Romford

Colchester Zoo

C olchester Zoo
O striches run,
L ions roar,
C heetahs run.
H yenas laugh,
E lephants stamp,
S nakes sliver,
T ortoises swim.
E mus are beautiful,
R unning reptiles,

Z ebras gallop,
O tters eat fish,
O ctopuses flow.

Ashleigh Doman (8)
St Edward's CE Primary School, Romford

The Rabbit And The Dog
(Inspired by 'The Owl and the Pussycat' by Edward Lear)

The rabbit and the dog went to Paris
In a soggy little lilypad boat
It didn't take long for it all to go wrong
So they both put on a furry coat.

Jack Blackman (8)
St Edward's CE Primary School, Romford

The Dog And The Hamster
(Inspired by 'The Owl and the Pussycat' by Edward Lear)

The dog and the hamster went to Southend
In a lovely pink super fast car
They took some honey and plenty of money
Which they put in a tiny blue jar.

Morwenna Masters (7)
St Edward's CE Primary School, Romford

The Highwayman

I saw the massive shadow gaining on us
With the horse pounding into the ground.
I looked out of the door,
There he was gun raised and masked. My heart was racing
I watched as he got closer and closer.

I could hear the hooves on the stony ground,
The horse snorting louder and louder,
The man breathing very heavily.
I heard the shot of a small gun,
Heard the bullet whistle past me.

I felt the vibration of the hooves and the tapping on the door.
I felt the end of a gun as it jabbed in my arm.
I felt my shivering body. My arm suddenly tensed.
I felt a gust of wind as another bullet whistled past me.
Then a slim bullet plunged into my tensed arm.
Sweat was dribbling down my neck - pain!

The taste from the dreadful gun.
I yelped as another bullet went straight in my belly.
I tasted the blood as it oozed out of my mouth,
Sick and vile.

That was when I smelt the stench of the huge man
As he reached across me and took my gold from my carriage.
That was when I noticed it was . . . the highwayman.

John Taylor (10)
St Edward's CE Primary School, Romford

Untitled

(Inspired by 'The Owl and the Pussycat' by Edward Lear)

The dog and the pig went up to space in a rocket
The rocket was big just like a pig
So they took it all in a bucket.

Andrew Frost (7)
St Edward's CE Primary School, Romford

The Dancer

I see a flock of people on the dance floor,
When I came in I heard lovely music
And suddenly my foot was tapping.

I began dancing and I felt happy inside,
Dancing like a beautiful butterfly.
I can feel a fresh warm breeze
Coming in from the open window.
All the people around me are talking,
Jumping, singing, shouting and running.

Modupe Gbadebo (10)
St Edward's CE Primary School, Romford

Fire

Fire makes me angry
Fire makes me hot
Fire makes me cry
It is hot, it is hot
Fire kills, I don't like it
It is horrible
I hate it
It is hot, it is hot
Help us, help us, we are dying.

Katie Ridout (9)
St Edward's CE Primary School, Romford

The Guinea Pig And Fish
(Inspired by 'The Owl and the Pussycat' by Edward Lear)

The guinea pig and fish went to Southend
In a tall fluffy orange crane
They took some money and a cute jumping bunny
But the bunny jumped into a lane.

Emily Massingham (7)
St Edward's CE Primary School, Romford

Fire

F ear in the smoke
I nside the crown of bright orange flames
R age of hotness
E ager to get out of the scared suit.

Vanessa Hamilton (9)
St Edward's CE Primary School, Romford

My Big Sister

My sister Rachel, is a girlie girl,
She likes to play with her curly curls.
She takes my things when I don't see,
But she likes to bother me.

Naomi Vallance (8)
St Edward's CE Primary School, Romford

The Slug And The Bug
(Inspired by 'The Owl and the Pussycat' by Edward Lear)

The slug and the bug went to the park
in a slimy buggy car.
They took some worms and some horrible germs
which they ate on the way to the park.

Bradley West (7)
St Edward's CE Primary School, Romford

The Rabbit And Hamster
(Inspired by 'The Owl and the Pussycat' by Edward Lear)

The rabbit and the hamster went to Paris
In a pea-green floating glass bottle
They took some peas and some very old bees
Which they stuffed in a boot with some nettles.

Jasmine Jennings (7)
St Edward's CE Primary School, Romford

The Dog And The Frog
(Inspired by'The Owl and the Pussycat' by Edward Lear)

The dog and the frog went to a log
In a bright red and green car
They took some crabs and some concrete slabs
Which they couldn't throw very far.

Charlotte Wickens (7)
St Edward's CE Primary School, Romford

The Slug And Bug

They went to the pub
And on the way, they saw a plane,
It flew to Disneyland
So it took a bunny which cried
Because it started to rain.

Daniel Balli (7)
St Edward's CE Primary School, Romford

The Cat In The Hat

The cat in the hat went to Southend,
In a new shiny zooming train,
They took some beans and a magazine
And they carried them all on the way.

Bethany Moore (7)
St Edward's CE Primary School, Romford

The Dog And The Hog
(Inspired by 'The Owl and the Pussycat' by Edward Lear)

The dog and the hog went to the log,
In a lovely fat red and green car,
They took some peas and some old cheese,
Which they stuffed in a marmalade jar.

Annabel Webb (8)
St Edward's CE Primary School, Romford

Climber

I'm a climber, climbing the slopes,
I can see the lions opening their jaws out wide,
Waiting for me to come closer,
I can see the rocks as sharp as daggers,
Waiting for me to come closer,
I can see snow wanting to trip me up,
Waiting for me to come closer.

I'm a climber, climbing the slopes,
Listening to the mountainside,
I can hear the lions roaring,
Listening to the mountain side,
I can hear the snow falling,
I'm listening to the mountainside noises.

I'm a climber, climbing the slopes,
Feeling the soft snow,
I can feel the sharp rocks,
I can feel the ice,
I'm the climber of the mountainside!

Maria Marks (10)
St Edward's CE Primary School, Romford

Graffiti Artist

When you are using a graffiti can on the wall
You see paint dripping down the wall,
Like custard dripping down a slice of apple pie.

You can hear the hissing of the can,
Shouts of people from the nearby pub,
Shotgun shots, fading into the dark, black night.

You feel your cold hand grasping onto the metal can,
You have the gun in your pocket,
Rubbing in the side of your hip,
You're feeling hot in the cold night.

Joel Poultney (10)
St Edward's CE Primary School, Romford

The Tornado

The tornado is twirling,
The lethal tornado.
It picks its victim,
Out of the five continents.
And once it has,
It strikes, like a chameleon's
Tongue catching a grasshopper.

The tornado sucks up all in its way,
It tears off the roof of the library
And sucks out all of the books.
It throws buses, lifts power stations and kills people.
It rips up trees like a girl picking a daisy
And drops them miles away.

What is left after a tornado?
Metal scraps, broken bricks and a faint outline
Of where a supermarket used to lie.
This is what a *tornado* can *cause*.

Sean Melpuss (10)
St Edward's CE Primary School, Romford

The Soldier

I can see the blasting bombs,
The thudding sound,
The way the planes soar over everyone's heads.

I can hear the slamming sounds of bombs,
I can hear the punching sounds of the bombs
And guns, the horrible sounds of tanks.

I can feel the sweat dropping down my head,
I can feel the squelching mud
And water under my boots.

I can smell the ashes burning in the distance,
I can smell the fire flaming up so far!
Fire! Fire! Fire!

Alana Speakman-Bell (10)
St Edward's CE Primary School, Romford

Music

I can see fans all going mad,
To only one word I speak.
I can see gangsters waiting for me to finish singing,
So that they can go in for the kill,
I can see the DJ turning up the background music.

Bones cracking as excited fans trample on each other,
Like a bull fight raging.
Gun shots as I remember the time
My best friend was lying right next to me.
I can hear cheers and some boos,
The loud camera sound.

I can feel the scare of fans that think the gangsters
Are coming after them.
I feel like the pain of not digesting my food
Has just come back again.
It makes me sick like a toad,
Coughing up a rotten fly,
But when I am back at home, I feel relaxed.

Oyinkansola Sunmonu (10)
St Edward's CE Primary School, Romford

Drummer

I see the people shouting and screaming,
Flashing lights in my eyes,
The sweat dripping down off my face like pouring rain.

I can hear the beat of the drum,
The string of the guitar,
The burps of the drunk and my
Voice into my microphone.

I can feel the vibration of the drum,
The tension in my limbs,
The nerves biting away,
My mind saying, *you can do it, you can do it!*

Callum James (10)
St Edward's CE Primary School, Romford

Runner, Running A Race

I can see the sun right in my eyes blinding me,
I can see the finish line right in front of me two metres away.

I can hear everyone cheering me on,
I can hear my family cheering and shouting, 'Go boy, go!'

I feel happiness running through my body,
I feel sweat running down my head.

I can taste sick coming up in my throat,
I can taste the sweat, it felt so cold,
Heart pumping, feet prancing, I'm there.
Winner!

Daisy Loomes (10)
St Edward's CE Primary School, Romford

Volcano

V anessa the volcano,
O h and don't touch,
L eave me alone,
C an you see I'm about to explode,
A very dangerous sight,
N ever touch, very hot,
O h have I said, 'My name is Vanessa!'

Amy Morrison (9)
St Edward's CE Primary School, Romford

The Cat In The Hat
(Inspired by 'The Owl and the Pussycat' by Edward Lear)

The cat in the hat went to a flat,
In a beautiful bright yellow car,
He took some cheese and
Got stung by some bees and
He then played the little guitar.

Sophie Tibbott (7)
St Edward's CE Primary School, Romford

Natives Attack

I can see arrows shooting across the lakes,
As campfires warm up the air,
Tents surround the forest the size of an evergreen tree.

I can hear drums pounding in the east,
As the troops come galloping towards the enemy
On white stallions at the speed of light.

I can feel rough land under my feet,
As I run from the ditch that was made by a furious cannonball,
I can feel my warm bloody hands as I attack the enemy,
Thud! Crash! is the sound as yet another man flies to the floor.

James Weimer (10)
St Edward's CE Primary School, Romford

Tornado

T urning around very fast,
O ver there,
R unning in the air,
N ow coming over here,
A nd be very careful,
D on't go too near,
O r you will get blown away!

Robert Carter (9)
St Edward's CE Primary School, Romford

Raindrops

I can hear the raindrops rushing down the road,
I can hear the rain running down my coat,
I can feel the raindrops splashing on my nose,
I can taste the raindrops dropping from my hair,
I can smell the raindrops tapping on the ground,
Raindrops everywhere.

Katharine Leonard (10)
St Edward's CE Primary School, Romford

In The Playground

I can see the children roaring in the playground,
Fast runners running in and out of people,
Waving trees, waving at the children,
Helpful teachers helping a hurting child,
Children throwing balls in the netball hoops,
Big buildings standing tall and stately,
Colourful footballs flying through the air,
Green gates being leant on by the children.

I can hear the sound of rustling trees in the distance,
I can hear all the noisy boys
And the sound of whistles blowing
People's feet pattering on the concrete floor.

I can feel the wind lightly blowing
And the pen in my hand,
I can smell the paint drying on the picture on the wall,
And the smell of my lunch box.

Zachary Trott (10)
St Edward's CE Primary School, Romford

Guitarist At Concert

I can see the dazzling lights in front of me,
The crowd as big as a gigantic black square,
The red face of the plectrum staring at me,
The black guitar catching the blue lights.

I can hear the loud screams of the crowd,
Like a loud speaker shouting out,
The strumming of the guitar growling like a bear,
The thumping of the lyrics in my ear.

I can feel the trembling of my arm,
Like the beating of the drum kit,
The thumping of my heart, like the beating of the speaker,
The sweat dripping off me,
Like the falling of the rain.

Lewis Huff (10)
St Edward's CE Primary School, Romford

The Rainforest

What I can see . . .
Trees with nests and birds eating
The river is splashing the crocodile
Bushes blocking my view
Crocodiles now snapping angrily.

What I can hear . . .
Birds singing to each other
River still splashing
Trees rustling in the wind
Crocodiles snapping, snapping, snapping ...

What I can smell and feel . . .
I can feel excitement but I am scared
I can smell the lovely fruit
I feel bark, it's fallen from the tree,
And there is the tree.

Callum Haxell (10)
St Edward's CE Primary School, Romford

A Rumbling Thought

E mbrace a sound of rubble,
A strange event awaits,
R umbling away near me it gets closer and closer,
T he noise is like an earthquake,
H old it, it is a loud booming noise,
   An earthquake must be near,
Q uaking through the stone,
U nder the ground it awaits,
A s swift as an explosion,
K now what is coming,
E rr, maybe ... it is my stomach.
   Hungry to eat ...
   Food!

Dominic Cheung (9)
St Edward's CE Primary School, Romford

Colour Ball

Red is the colour of a rose,
Orange is the colour of a big hairy nose.
Yellow is just like the sun,
Green is just super fun.
Blue is the colour of the sky,
Purple is like a hover fly.
Pink is the prettiest of them all,
That's the end of the colour ball.

Rosie Webber (8)
St Edward's CE Primary School, Romford

Volcano

V olcano means,
O h no exploding,
L ook volcanoes are so bright,
C razy people,
A movement on the ground,
N o it is all too much,
O h boy it is hot.

Alex Cutmore (9)
St Edward's CE Primary School, Romford

My Fire

Boys are really annoying especially my little brothers
But they live in Spain with my dad,
When boys annoy me, I feel like fire is coming out of my ears,
And sometimes I feel like I'm going to fly up to Mars,
Be an astronaut and be the first person to walk on Mars,
That's funny because in my classroom
I'm listening to Star Wars, the song and my teacher is singing it.

Rosie Louise White (9)
St Edward's CE Primary School, Romford

Hamsters Can . . .

Hamsters can run,
Hamsters are sneaky.
They are greedy,
Hamster are very noisy.
Hamsters can bite,
Hamsters can jump.
Hamster can climb,
Hamsters can be very fast,
Hamsters are very messy.

Christopher Attridge (8)
St Edward's CE Primary School, Romford

School

School is great, school is fun,
School is good for everyone,
You learn your lessons one by one.
Maths, literacy and lots of history,
Art is funky, gluey and sticky,
Painting lots of fingerprints and colourful paint.
At the end of the day I'm exhausted,
But always want to go back tomorrow.

Hannah King (9)
St Edward's CE Primary School, Romford

Flood

F ear all around us,
L ife being taken,
O ver cars and lorries,
O ver the treetop it goes,
D rowning people on its way.

Elizabeth Gregory (9)
St Edward's CE Primary School, Romford

The Season's Garden

It's the first season of the year
It's spring
The flowers bloom all different colours
Pink, red, white, purple, yellow, orange and blue
There are different beautiful flowers
There are daisies, pansies, roses, poppies, daffodils and sunflowers,
All these colourful flowers surround me,
Like a flower house keeping me warm
And then we move onto summer
It's nice and hot
As I sit under a big tree,
I see people go to the pool
As I am enjoying the summer sun
I love to have a picnic in the summer under my favourite tree
As I hear the birds sing a song and I enjoy the bumblebee.
I can see the honeybee do a dance
I can see the beehive living its chance from the hot summer
I have to put on my suncream or I'll get burnt.
As we move on into autumn, as the leaves fall down from the trees,
All colourful leaves rain the air the colours fill me with
joy and happiness,
We are all getting ready for winter and as we move on
Into winter, my favourite season as all the trees are covered in snow
And my mum is stuffing the Christmas turkey,
My dad is enjoying Christmas carols and I am outside
Making a snowman, the day has come to open my presents
And have the Christmas turkey but then the snow dies
Down and we all start all over again.

Temi Abatan (8)
St Edward's CE Primary School, Romford

Bubbles

The bubble floats in the air
and has a soft pop
and little bubble flies again.

Fraser Scott (7)
St Edward's CE Primary School, Romford

Hurricane

Hurricanes are scary and terrifying.
Underneath the covers I hide because I'm scared and terrified.
Wrecking things is what hurricanes like to do.
Wreck everything.
I can hear babies crying, mums screaming.
Crying and screaming
And your house is ruined.
Near a hurricane you feel scared, worried, terrified.
Everything is ruined.

Betsey Benson (9)
St Edward's CE Primary School, Romford

Football

F abulous football
O ver the goal the ball goes
O h no! I missed
T he fans boo
B ang! The ball went on a footballer's head
A nd the ball goes to the goal
L ucky goal!
L ove football.

Emmanuel Olusanya (9)
St Edward's CE Primary School, Romford

The Croc And The Dog
(Inspired by 'The Owl and the Pussycat' by Edward Lear)

The croc and the dog
Went to a log,
In a bright yellow plane,
They took some logs with a bottle of frogs
And ate them on the train.

Kimberley Stirk (8)
St Edward's CE Primary School, Romford

A To Z Of Animals

A nthea the antelope is running very fast
B illy the billy goat is munching on the grass
C hloe the chestnut pony is giving a child a ride
D aisy the dolphin is swimming in the ocean
E ric the elephant is raising his trunk
F raser the fish is playing with his friends
G eorgina the giraffe is very, very tall
H annah the hare is hiding in her house
I saac the icy penguin is freezing cold
J acob the jaguar is sleeping in his den
K errie the koala is climbing up the tree
L ola the lion is looking at her hair
M elanie the monkey is swinging from tree to tree
N icholas the nice cheetah is searching for something to eat
O liver the octopus is squeezing other sea animals
P eter the python is slithering all around
Q ueen of the bees is buzzing all around
R oger the rhino is very fat
S ally the snail is cleaning her shell
T homas the turtle is in the water
U ranus the unicorn is showing off her lovely body
V ictoria the vulture is eating human flesh
W illiam the whale is squirting water from his back
X odus the X-ray-eyed rabbit is looking at people's bones
Y oda the yak is eating a lot
Z ena the zebra has got lovely black and white stripes.

Kerrie Norris (8)
St Edward's CE Primary School, Romford

Flood

F loods are very dangerous,
L ike a fire,
O ther
O fficial, this is a
D angerous volcano.

George Zuber (9)
St Edward's CE Primary School, Romford

In My Cousin's Bedroom (A-Z)

A crobats (to learn some exercises)
B at (to scare people)
C at (to scratch invaders)
D racula (to suck people's blood)
E ggs and spoons (to race against time)
F ish (to fry at lunchtime)
G oat (to wash her clothes)
H at (that can change)
I guana (she's a bit of a science freak)
J elly (for secret sleepovers)
K ing (she likes to be royal)
L emon (it makes her go crazy)
M onkey (to get in the swing)
N ecklace (to dance with the king)
O ctopus (to do the housework)
P uppy (to cuddle at bedtime)
Q ueen (to dance with the king)
R ug (to lie on)
S nail (to do things quickly)
T oys (to play with when she's in bed)
U gly bug (to go to the ball)
V ole (to look after)
W ater (last night's drink)
X ylophone (from the percussion band)
Y ak (from the Spanish farm)
Z oo (elephants as well).

Aimee Harvey (8)
St Edward's CE Primary School, Romford

The Dog And The Cat
(Inspired by 'The Owl and the Pussycat' by Edward Lear)

The dog and the cat sat on the mat,
In a gorgeous shiny red car,
They had some peas and some smelly cheese,
On the way they both played guitar.

Rachael John (7)
St Edward's CE Primary School, Romford

A To Z Of Animals

A is for the antelope running swiftly through the grass
B is for the bird flying up above
C is for the cat jumping road to road
D is for the deer galloping in the woods
E is for the elephant splashing in the rain
F is for the fish swimming smoothly through the sea
G is for the giraffe with its neck up in space
H is for the hippo diving in the sea
I is for the iguana hanging in the trees
K is for the kangaroos bouncing up and down
L is for the leopard leaping in the forest
M is for the monkey swinging tree to tree
N is for the newt jumping on the lilies
O is for the octopus stretching up and down
P is for the penguin waddling on the ice
Q is for the queen bee buzzing on the leaves
R is for the rhino fighting with its horn
S is for the snake slithering on the leaves
T is for the tiger munching on its mat
U is for the unicorn charging in the dust
V is for the vole digging in the dirt
W is for the walrus paddling in the water
X is for the xenopus soaking in the rain
Y is for the yak shedding in the dark
Z is for zebra running on the grass.

Adam Ward (8)
St Edward's CE Primary School, Romford

The Cat And The Hat

(Inspired by 'The Owl and the Pussycat' by Edward Lear)

The cat and the hat went to Paris,
In a super huge white limousine,
They took some berries and some juicy cherries,
Which they decided to name Bob and Dean.

Liam Chesney (8)
St Edward's CE Primary School, Romford

Animals And Pets (A-Z)

A nimals can be from the wild and some from pet shops
B aboons are from the wild and they like bananas
C ats can come in big and small and they like to drink milk
D ogs drink water and they like to fetch
E lephants have long trunks
F oxes feast on chicken
G uinea pigs' fur is very smooth
H yenas love to eat fresh meat
I guanas like to hiss at you
J aguars hunt with their teeth and claws
K oalas like to climb up trees
L eopards like to jump up trees
M oths like to fly up high
N anny goats nibble lots of grass
O ctopuses have long and sticky tentacles
P enguins like to eat big fish
Q uails fly up in the sky
R ats like to bite some things
S quirrels like to run up trees
T igers eat tons of meat
U nderwater animals are mostly fish
V ultures are very vicious
W hales are very big
X -ray fish are very skinny
Y aks are very fast
Z ebras are very stripy.

Thomas Steer (8)
St Edward's CE Primary School, Romford

Floods

F earing people everywhere,
L ots of people running everywhere,
O ver many treetops,
O ver buildings,
D rawing people short and tall on their way.

Alice Rayment-Smith (9)
St Edward's CE Primary School, Romford

Tornado

Tornado, tornado,
Round you go
You make the seas and trees blow,
If you're not already dead,
Then your life is hanging by a thread.

Savanna Rayment (9)
St Edward's CE Primary School, Romford

Fire, Fire

There's a fire in town,
I will admire you if you save him now.
Maybe you could pour a bucket of water to stop the fire,
Fire, fire you stopped the fire,
Fire, fire you are the one who I'm going to admire.

Victor Olusina (9)
St Edward's CE Primary School, Romford

The Lonely Moonlight

The lonely moonlight saw seven silver silky wolves
Shivering in the cold night air,
Howling tuneless tunes!

The moonlight flashed through opened doors
Peeping at everything its lonely eyes could see!

Kane Chandler (10)
St Edward's CE Primary School, Romford

My Budgie

My budgie, he glimmers and glides in the air,
And stops to stretch his wings
And have little nibbles.

Beau Avis (9)
St Edward's CE Primary School, Romford

Strawberry

S mall and sour
T asty and sweet
R ed
A nd ripe
W ith cream I taste
B rilliant and
E xcellent
R ed, ripe and
R ound
Y ummy!

Jade Hill (8)
St Edward's CE Primary School, Romford

Rabbit Cage

Rabbits are fun,
Rabbits can dance,
Rabbits can sing in the night sky.
Rabbits can twirl,
Rabbits can bounce,
Rabbits like to jump up and down.
Rabbits love to hop
And run around.

Charlotte Neale (8)
St Edward's CE Primary School, Romford

Rabbit

R eally good muncher
A pples (I love them)
B ananas (like them)
B ed (sleeps in)
I (love my rabbit)
T oys (plays with them).

Chloe Haxell (8)
St Edward's CE Primary School, Romford

Guess Who?

Claw pincher
Eye winker
Side walker
Non talker
Large claws
Scary jaws
Lives in sand
When on land
Hard shell
Fishy smell.

What am I?

Holly Brown (8)
St Edward's CE Primary School, Romford

Christmas

Christmas cheer,
Christmas trees,
Christmas everywhere.

Christmas near,
Christmas presents,
But the best part is the Christmas dinner.

Oliver Portway (8)
St Edward's CE Primary School, Romford

Guess Who?

Fluffy-wuffy
Bushy tail
Right thumper
Carrot muncher
Fast runner.
Who am I?

Ruby Ison (8)
St Edward's CE Primary School, Romford

My Friend, Madeleine

M adeleine is kind
A lovely girl
D aring she is
E legant dress she has
L ie, she does not
E ating is a problem
I n clean condition
N asty she isn't
E verlasting friendship!

Bethany Eades (8)
St Edward's CE Primary School, Romford

Disneyland

Lots of rides,
Lots of fun,
What shall we go on,
Which one?
There's *Mission Space* and the *Twilight Zone*
And *Star Tours* and *Pluto* with a bone!
Shall we go on *Tower of Terror?*
Ahhh!

Nathan Smith (8)
St Edward's CE Primary School, Romford

The Eagle And The Raven

(Inspired by 'The Owl and the Pussycat' by Edward Lear)

The eagle and the raven went to town
In a pink spotty caravan
They took some money
And plenty of honey
So they never made a sound again.

Emily Eglinton (7)
St Edward's CE Primary School, Romford

The Moon And The Stars

The stars are good to look at
They're really really bright.
The stars are good to look at
I watch them all the night.
I like to watch the moon as well
It seems like it swells and swells.
I really like the moon with the background of the night
That sometimes gives me a fright.

Luke Sheridan (8)
St Edward's CE Primary School, Romford

Lollipop

It's sticky,
messy and
ice-cold
and yummy,
gooey
and
an
ice
pop.

Bethany Greene (7)
St Edward's CE Primary School, Romford

Bubble

Bubbles fly up into the sky over the roofs
Pop, pop, pop over the highway
Onto the car park,
Pop, pop, pop.

Edward Brinton-Quinn (7)
St Edward's CE Primary School, Romford

Lion And Cheetah

(Inspired by 'The Owl and the Pussycat' by Edward Lear)

The lion and cheetah went to Spain,
One day in a golden racing car.
They took some money
And some honey too.
When they got there it was very hot
But then they found water in a pot.
It was still too hot, then they fainted,
While a painter painted them
The lion caught the flu.

Fishomi Lawal (7)
St Edward's CE Primary School, Romford

Bubbles

Floating bubbles in the air
Floating bubbles everywhere
Magically moving in your hair
Gently popping in the air
Shining rainbow colours
Glistening through the air
Soapy water everywhere
Floating up in the air.

Faith Howard (8)
St Edward's CE Primary School, Romford

The Bug And The Bat

(Inspired by 'The Owl and the Pussycat' by Edward Lear)

The bug and the bat went to a cave
In a really fat flying melon
They took some blood and a load of mud
With a really yummy lemon.

Daniel Fajinmi (8)
St Edward's CE Primary School, Romford

The Rabbit And The Kitten
(Inspired by 'The Owl and the Pussycat' by Edward Lear)

The rabbit and the kitten went to town,
In a red and blue convertible.
They got out of the car and fell on a chocolate bar
And ate it all up, yum-yum.

Ethan Shepherd (7)
St Edward's CE Primary School, Romford

The Owl And The Raven
(Inspired by 'The Owl and the Pussycat' by Edward Lear)

The owl and the raven went to sea,
On a pink and green buzzy bee.
They took some mice and some spice
For their lovely day at sea.

Linus Leung (7)
St Edward's CE Primary School, Romford

Long Puffer

Long puffer
Fast runner
Licker, flicker
Sucker supper
Good pouncer.
Who am I?

Victoria Hall (8)
St Edward's CE Primary School, Romford

The Cat And A Rat

(Inspired by 'The Owl and the Pussycat' by Edward Lear)

The cat and a rat got to Greece
In an amazing, super-fast car.
They took some mice and lots of rice
And instead they made it to Mars.

Samuel Quang (8)
St Edward's CE Primary School, Romford

The Cat And The Dog

(Inspired by 'The Owl and the Pussycat' by Edward Lear)

The cat and the dog went for a jog
And on the way they saw a fox.
It was doing a jig with a silly green wig
While a chicken was trapped in a box.

Monika Degun (7)
St Edward's CE Primary School, Romford

The Cat And The Dog

(Inspired by 'The Owl and the Pussycat' by Edward Lear)

The cat and the dog went to Mars
In a spotty banana boat
And took some honey and a lot of money
And had a yummy bar and said,
'Ha, ha,' to a goat.

James Bastick (7)
St Edward's CE Primary School, Romford

The Alligator And The Crocodile

(Inspired by 'The Owl and the Pussycat' by Edward Lear)

The alligator and the crocodile went to Saturn
In a spotty blue van.
They saw some stars and chocolate bars
As they got a tan.

Jack Rich (7)
St Edward's CE Primary School, Romford

The Dog And The Frog

(Inspired by 'The Owl and the Pussycat' by Edward Lear)

The dog and the frog went to a log
And rode on a big fat giraffe.
They took a great giant and made him a lion
But they couldn't escape from his laugh.

Chloe Baisden (7)
St Edward's CE Primary School, Romford

The Cat And The Rat

(Inspired by 'The Owl and the Pussycat' by Edward Lear)

The cat and the rat went to a flat
In a blue, yellow and red car.
They took some red cheese
And some lovely green beans
With marmalade squashed in a jam jar.

Amelia Grocock (7)
St Edward's CE Primary School, Romford

The Slug And The Bug

(Inspired by 'The Owl and the Pussycat' by Edward Lear)

The slug and the bug went to Spain
In a big, pink, fluffy plane
They took some mugs and lots of bugs
Which they dropped on a fast passing train.

Olivia Kavanagh (7)
St Edward's CE Primary School, Romford

The Giraffe And The Dog

(Inspired by 'The Owl and the Pussycat' by Edward Lear)

The giraffe and the dog went to France
In a very bright red speedboat.
They took some peas
And got stung by some bees
And got trapped by a big billy goat.

David Goff (7)
St Edward's CE Primary School, Romford

The Horse And The Snake

(Inspired by 'The Owl and the Pussycat' by Edward Lear)

The horse and the snake went to a lake
And got stuffed in a green and black taxi
They took some dead rats and some nasty small gnats
But their ears turned out to be waxy.

Emma Whitby (8)
St Edward's CE Primary School, Romford

The Lurcher

The dog was running in the park
He was running really quick,
He played with a poodle
And didn't want to go home,
His owner said, 'Five more minutes.'
So he was happy,
But still he didn't want to go home.

Sam Blowers (10)
St Edward's CE Primary School, Romford

The Illness Called The Flush

The dog and the toilet were talking loudly
In the bathroom proudly
The dog took some toilet paper and a shoe
The toilet got the flush
And hit him with the toilet brush.

Daniella Anderson (9)
St Edward's CE Primary School, Romford

The Dog And The Frog

(Inspired by 'The Owl and the Pussycat' by Edward Lear)

The dog and the frog went to the log
In a nice yellow car
They took some beef and some beans
Which they stuffed in a marmalade jar.

Francesca Cutmore (7)
St Edward's CE Primary School, Romford

Splash!

The orange fox ran quickly through the park,
Running away from the fat park keeper,
A girl dropped her banana skin,
The fox dodged it,
The park keeper slipped on it
Then he fell in the pond!
        Splash!

Emma Hatwell (9)
St Edward's CE Primary School, Romford

The Pig And The Pigeon
(Inspired by 'The Owl and the Pussycat' by Edward Lear)

The pig and the pigeon ran to market
To buy what they could buy
Along came a beast and grabbed the pigeon and said,
'Tonight I'll eat bird and fries.'

Samuel Cockburn (9)
St Edward's CE Primary School, Romford

The Mouse And The Elephant
(Inspired by 'The Owl and the Pussycat' by Edward Lear)

The mouse and the elephant went to Spain,
On a blue spotty jet-ski,
They paid some money for a live mummy,
They were never ever seen again.

Jack Herbert (10)
St Edward's CE Primary School, Romford

The Bear And The Mermaid

(Inspired by 'The Owl and the Pussycat' by Edward Lear)

The bear and the mermaid took a trip to France
They rode on a white stallion all the way
They took a bath and lots of water and a cake for tea
They went away and never came back.

Molly Keir (9)
St Edward's CE Primary School, Romford

The Pig And The Cat

(Inspired by 'The Owl and the Pussycat' by Edward Lear)

The pig and the cat got into their boat
And sailed off to Spain.
They took two things with them
A football and candles
And they were never seen again.

Alice Pugh (9)
St Edward's CE Primary School, Romford

The Monkey And The Horse

(Inspired by 'The Owl and the Pussycat' by Edward Lear)

The monkey and the horse went to Italy
In a nice big, green galleon.
They took some fast food, salad, vodka
And got drunk and started to fight.

Alexander Hardy (9)
St Edward's CE Primary School, Romford

The Pig And The Elephant

(Inspired by 'The Owl and the Pussycat' by Edward Lear)

The elephant and the pig went to Spain,
They went on a blue aeroplane,
But the pig jumped out of it
And landed on the ground.

Maddison Gilbey (9)
St Edward's CE Primary School, Romford

The Hamster And The Dog

(Inspired by 'The Owl and the Pussycat' by Edward Lear)

The hamster and the dog went to Spain
In a bright green spotted boat
They took a sandwich and a bottle of beer
And fell out of the side.

Abbie Legallienne (9)
St Edward's CE Primary School, Romford

The Mouse And The Pussycat

(Inspired by 'The Owl and the Pussycat' by Edward Lear)

The mouse and the pussycat went to France
Luckily they were in first class
The mouse was happy, the pussycat was not
So the cat threw the mouse into the sea
The mouse was never, ever, ever, ever seen again.

Saffron Robins (9)
St Edward's CE Primary School, Romford

Volcano

Volcanoes are full of ash.
Volcanoes can kill.
Vibration, wish could stop.
Hot, red, burning,
Burning makes me angry.
Wish could stop.
Larvary!

Ben Austin (9)
St Edward's CE Primary School, Romford

The Pig And The Wolf
(Inspired by 'The Owl and the Pussycat' by Edward Lear)

A pig and a wolf went in a rowing boat
They got tickets and went to the fair
They had a big pear all round and juicy and fat
They went home feeling very sick.

Gemma Willson (9)
St Edward's CE Primary School, Romford

Cat And Rat
(Inspired by 'The Owl and the Pussycat' by Edward Lear)

A cat and a rat driving in a cab
When they got there
The cat said to the rat,
'Would you dare to have a flap like mine?'

Amy Picknell (7)
St Edward's CE Primary School, Romford

Tornado

T wisting and turning,
O ver and over again.
R ound and round,
N asty winds,
A ble to destroy.
D oing its worst,
O ver and over again.

Bruce Beckett (9)
St Edward's CE Primary School, Romford

Colours

Pink and green and black, that's mean.
Orange and yellow and white, that can bellow.
Purple and pink and dark staining ink.
Silver and gold, that is very bold.
Me and you we both go boo
Because sadly this poem is finished.

Karen Morris (8)
St Edward's CE Primary School, Romford

A Rat And A Bat

(Inspired by 'The Owl and the Pussycat' by Edward Lear)

A rat and a bat
driving a car
took a bun
and on the way
they found a gun.

Joshua Amofah (7)
St Edward's CE Primary School, Romford

Rainforest

What can I see?
The bright beautiful birds singing in the trees,
The stream with the sun reflecting in it,
The holly bush and the berry bush,
And a path for me to walk on.

The monkeys swinging swiftly,
To the gorillas sitting there grumpily
Under the big bright tree
Where the ants have made their nest.

What can I hear?
The gorillas growling grumpily
The crunching of the leaves
The bees making honey
And the rustling of the trees.

Sophie Doyle (10)
St Edward's CE Primary School, Romford

Jupiter

Jupiter, the king of the planets.
Bigger than a giant.
Red, orange and yellow stripes and swirls.
A ball of gas,
Burning hot,
Like fire burning all the time.
The colours beaming,
What a fantastic planet,
But the question I want to find out
Is why is it so great?

Jessica Stephenson (9)
The Bishops' CE & RC (VA) Primary School

Space Poem

5, 4, 3, 2, 1, here I go
Launching out of extreme Earth
And heading to mini Mars.
Shhhh, go the meteor showers
And the asteroids too.
Boy it's as dark as a jaguar,
I never knew space was so empty,
It's as empty as a deserted island.

Saad Malik (10)
The Bishops' CE & RC (VA) Primary School

Stars

Stars so bright all through the night.
Together or apart with their little light.
What is it like up there with stars so bright?
Is it pretty or is it dull?
The stars are bright all through the night
When you look in the night sky
You see the stars falling from the sky,
Like pretty little snowflakes with bright little lights.

Ellie Fivash (10)
The Bishops' CE & RC (VA) Primary School

Space

Space, oh space, the wonderful pace of the rocket,
Flying through the stars, as fast as cars.
Space, oh space, the stars in space
You twinkle far and wide.
Space, oh space, your planets race
They've been there thousands of years.
Space, space, yes I know,
Somebody will come back so, yes I know.

Joshua Fresle (9)
The Bishops' CE & RC (VA) Primary School

Space

Apollo 11, Apollo 13
Neil Armstrong and Buzz Aldrin
Went into space, onto the moon,
Came back to Earth sooner than soon.

Saturn, Pluto and Mars
Different constellations for stars
We're getting closer to the sun
We don't want to get burnt so run, run, run.

The sun is the red warrior
And it's got the hottest core
Even my spaceship
Can't touch its tip.

Though I want to stay
I've got to go away
I hope I'll be back
To this paradise of black.

John Akomolafe (9)
The Bishops' CE & RC (VA) Primary School

Off I Go

Off I go to outer space,
On a mission to find a place.

That no one has been to before,
Off I go, 1, 2, 3, 4.

I saw Uranus, Venus and Mars,
One of them sounds like a chocolate bar!

As I went on I saw a bold star,
And driving around it was a small black car.

I flew around till I found the sun,
Flying in space is a big load of fun!

Off I go, back to Earth,
My wonderful, great place of birth!

Olivia Robinson (9)
The Bishops' CE & RC (VA) Primary School

Mission To The Stars

See the Milky Way, all so bright,
And look at the stars in the night,
Pegasus the horse,
Cancer the crab,
Scorpio the scorpion,
I feel so glad.
In my rocket heading further into space,
I feel so great, this is ace.
Marvellous Mars,
Giant Jupiter,
Where can we go.
Super Saturn,
Upside down Uranus.
Put the brakes on, let's slow.
Such a great time in the stars,
Next time I'll go to Mars.

Ellen Battye (9)
The Bishops' CE & RC (VA) Primary School

The Moon

The moon is so bright
Lights up the whole of the night.
As bright as the light of the sun.
The snowstorm is rough
A really snowy place,
The wind blows across
My freezing face
And the dark sky
That makes me feel
Like I could fly.
There was a crash
And a great big flash of lightning.
No cars,
Only twinkling stars.

Rebecca Scott (9)
The Bishops' CE & RC (VA) Primary School

Look At The Stars

Look at the stars,
Look at the stars;
Shining,
Shimmering,
Up in the heavens,
With all their glory.

Look at the stars,
Look at the stars;
Twinkling,
Glittering,
Up in the heavens,
With all their pride.

Look at the stars,
Look at the stars;
Glowing,
Gleaming,
Up in the heavens,
With all their light.

Phoebe Scherer (9)
The Bishops' CE & RC (VA) Primary School

The Race To Space

The race to space
And I brought my suitcase.
I saw Mars, Jupiter and Saturn.
Suddenly I don't know why
But I landed in the sky.
One second later, I was overtaken
So now I needed to race to space.
In the end the man who won,
Never saw his face
He was called, 'Mace'.

Samuel Ashford (9)
The Bishops' CE & RC (VA) Primary School

Hurry Up Neil Armstrong

Neil Armstrong getting ready
Feeling hot, like a cup of tea.

Wondering what to do in space,
First he'll ride the space buggy.

Everyone chasing after him,
Shouting, 'Neil, we don't have time!'

'I just need to write a plan or list.'
'Neil,' they used to whine.

He climbed into the space rocket
Feeling rather hot.

Off goes the radio, 5, 4, 3, 2, 1, blast off.
According to the plan or list that he left at home.

He refused to ride the space buggy,
'It's going too fast,' he moaned.

I'm heading home finally
The flag was planted well.

The footprints marked out on the moon,
I'll remember them so well.

Those sparkly dots up in the sky,
Oh I do love the stars.

My favourite planet of them all
Is fiery, bright red Mars.

Frances Stacey (9)
The Bishops' CE & RC (VA) Primary School

Mission To Space

5, 4, 3, 2, 1
This is going to be fun
I'm going up to space
You should see the look on my face.
I'm passing the stars, I'm going to Mars
Then I'll go to Saturn
The beautiful five-ringed Saturn.
Up above me twinkling in dim light are stars,
Libra,
Scorpio,
North Star.
I don't know where else to go,
Marvellous Mars,
Giant Jupiter,
Puny Pluto,
Oh, I don't know.

Ashley Lumayag (10)
The Bishops' CE & RC (VA) Primary School

The Weather Is Blue

The weather is blue
The weather is ooh
There are so many things about it
The weather is grey
It can rain night and day
When the sun comes up
The children all shout, 'Hooray!'

Anna Birmingham (7)
The Bishops' CE & RC (VA) Primary School

Space Poem

Shuttle I look at your huge engine.
Will you take me to Pluto?
I took off with a *bang!*
Here I go.
Sun,
Mercury,
Venus,
Mars.
Jupiter is made of gas which gives it its gigantic mass.
Saturn brightens up all other things.
Uranus, the only planet on its side.
Neptune, the 2nd most colourful planet in our universe.
Pluto, here I am.
I've landed.
The smallest of them all.
It is freezing cold.
Colder than the North Pole.

Peter Bowdidge (9)
The Bishops' CE & RC (VA) Primary School

Space, Space

Space, oh space
Your wonderful pace
Of the rockets flying to the moon.
The stars twinkling in my face
And glistening in my eyes,
Like the sun blinding me.

Space, oh space
There once was a race
To get the first man on the moon.
Space, space,
Yes I know somebody
Will come back here
So here we go.

Shannon O'Sullivan (9)
The Bishops' CE & RC (VA) Primary School

Space Race

5, 4, 3, 2, 1
Let's go to space
And have some fun.
I see the sun burning on Mars
But Pluto is the furthest from the stars.
Oh my gosh, a comet is coming my way.
If it hits me
It's going to pay!

Megan Norrington (10)
The Bishops' CE & RC (VA) Primary School

Space Poem

Rocket, rocket,
I stand in front of you.
I stare at your powerful armour.
Rocket, rocket,
Where shall I go?
What shall I do?
How about the asteroid belt?
So slowly it flows.

Matthew Allen (9)
The Bishops' CE & RC (VA) Primary School

Pluto

Pluto the deserted planet,
Sharp, cold and spiky.
Quiet, icy and bare,
Rocky like a steep mountain.
Pluto, the furthest planet from the sun,
That is why it is so cold, blue and freezing.
It has snow storms every single day,
The smallest planet, as rough as a goat's tongue.

Louise Palmer (9)
The Bishops' CE & RC (VA) Primary School

The Sun

The sun is an enormous star,
You can see it from afar.
You're not there at night,
Because you're tucked up tight.
Oh Sun, oh Sun.

You're so bright,
I wish you were there at night.
You're always burning,
But never turning,
Oh Sun, oh Sun.

Bethany Lodge (9)
The Bishops' CE & RC (VA) Primary School

Jupiter

Jupiter, the stormy planet
Jupiter, the giant planet
As colourful as a rainbow
As deadly as a tiger,
The noise of the engine, as hot as the sun
A scorching planet, made of gas
The atmosphere full of heat
Deserted as it may be
But as dangerous as a bomb.

Alex Woolnough (9)
The Bishops' CE & RC (VA) Primary School

Mars

Mars is hot, red and rocky.
Deserted, dark and dull, like a lonely corner.
It makes me feel like I'm there,
In the corner everywhere.

Joseph Brenchley (9)
The Bishops' CE & RC (VA) Primary School

Stars

Gazing up into space,
Stars all around.
Massive dull ones
And tiny sparkling ones, twirling
Like a great silver merry-go-round.
I feel like just reaching up
And pulling it right to the ground
Because what I see from down here
Is a story to be found.

Ella Beadel (10)
The Bishops' CE & RC (VA) Primary School

Up In Space And Beyond

Up in space, what do I see?
The bright, fiery sun and its flames shining on the planets.
Order from the sun, Mercury, Venus, Earth and Mars,
Jupiter, Uranus, Neptune and Pluto.
Furthest from the sun, poor Pluto.
Poor Pluto, so cold,
As it freezes the others tease it.
While Pluto stays by himself and thinks
That one day he will still be known as a planet.

Caitlin Sheehan (9)
The Bishops' CE & RC (VA) Primary School

The Sun

The sun, hot as can be,
But will never harm me.
Flames, orange, yellow and red,
Flying in spirals all over the place.
All colours flying into outer space!

Courtney Burnette (10)
The Bishops' CE & RC (VA) Primary School

Pluto

Grey, cold Pluto, going round on its own
No one wants to be there,
Too cold,
Too lonely,
As spiky as a needle,
Too small, too far,
Pluto's moon Charon, about half its size,
Too small, very small, too lonely,
No one ever goes to Pluto and its lonely moon.

Esther Daniel (9)
The Bishops' CE & RC (VA) Primary School

Pluto In Space

Icy, cold and freezing
Mate, there's no teasing!
It's a deserted kind of place
That spins around in space.
Year of 248
It takes to rotate
Scientists say it's not true
Because of the size,
So is it just all lies?

Georgia Hammond (10)
The Bishops' CE & RC (VA) Primary School

Jupiter

The air was clear on this dark, dark night
As Jupiter swayed there, left to right
A red, a pink, a purple, a blue
Was glowing in the light of the shining moon
Then it stopped really stiff, as it turned to midnight
Never again in the dark, dark night.

Sinead Collins (10)
The Bishops' CE & RC (VA) Primary School

The Spaceship

I saw a spaceship
Rush through the sky
I jumped on board
And I started to fly.

On board was an alien
With big friendly eyes
He said, 'Come with me
And eat space pies.'

We flew to the moon
To have some fun,
It was made of cheese
And I ate a tonne!

We flew past planets
And far into space
We saw another spaceship
And had a race.

We went too fast
I started to scream
But then I woke up
It was only a dream!

Sophie Parker (7)
The Bishops' CE & RC (VA) Primary School

The Stars

The stars sparkle with the misty moon,
Glowing and glowing with a little tune.
They're bright and warm and look so nice,
They're wonderful but look like mice.
Shooting through space as quick as can be,
It's just like a colourful fantasy.

Abigail Mariner (9)
The Bishops' CE & RC (VA) Primary School